The Power Dynamics

Author: Hannes van Zyl

Exploring the Top and Bottom Division

The Power Dynamics: Exploring the Top and Bottom Division

Email: Authorhannesvanzyl@gmail.com

Pretoria

Gauteng

South Africa

Introduction

Growing up on a farm in the Northern Cape, there wasn't much for a gay teenager to learn about being gay. The primary understanding we had was limited, with the hairdresser and the florist often being the only openly gay figures in our small community, serving as our sole representation. Beyond these individuals, there was scant information available, leaving us in a profound void regarding our identities. As a typical farm boy in the early 80s, I never imagined embodying the flamboyant behaviour often associated with openly gay individuals. It simply wasn't part of my self-identity, nor did I see it as a possibility for myself.

From an early age, I grasped one crucial truth: I am a man who loves men, and I want to remain a man. The idea of altering my identity as a man never crossed my mind then, and it absolutely doesn't today. I felt a strong sense of self that was rooted in my understanding of masculinity, and that was enough for me.

I believed that to attract a man, one had to resemble a woman. It was a time when the only openly gay individuals did not present themselves as traditional men, which added to the confusion and uncertainty surrounding our identities. What I didn't recognize was the reality that many gay men were living dual lives, kissing girls in public while engaging with men behind closed doors. This was the complicated, often painful landscape we had to navigate during those years, where the fear of judgment loomed large and pervasive, creating an atmosphere of silence and denial.

Today, the landscape is vastly different. I genuinely believe it's easier for younger generations to explore their identities freely and openly, without the same level of fear and shame that once held us back. This book isn't primarily about the journey of coming out as gay; instead, it delves into the often troubling and divisive split between tops and bottoms, a division that causes significant distress and confusion within the gay community, creating rifts that can be difficult to bridge.

Regarding the gay community, just for clarification: Definitions from Oxford Languages define gay as sexually or romantically attracted to people of one's own sex, typically applied to men. This is the context in which I refer to gay individuals throughout this book, as it forms the foundation of my understanding.

I recognize that many different identities exist within the expansive LGBTQ+ spectrum, and I don't presume to have informed opinions on their lifestyle choices or preferences since I lack sufficient knowledge in those areas. Each identity carries its own unique challenges and triumphs that I cannot fully comprehend or articulate. Will they find value in this book? I believe they might, and I sincerely hope so, although I can't predict their individual experiences with its content. All I can do is offer my unwavering support and understanding, hoping that my perspective resonates with some, even if only a few.

I hope that today's young gay individuals can look around and see that role models are now far more visible than the few I encountered in my youth. It is our responsibility as a community to ensure that we do not fail the younger generation; we must step up and exemplify what it means to be ordinary gay men living purposeful, authentic lives. We should strive to serve as beacons of hope and inspiration for those who follow in our footsteps, guiding them toward a future where they can embrace their identities without fear and with pride, knowing they are not alone on their journey.

Acknowledgments

To my Heavenly Father, I am profoundly grateful for the incredible grace and unwavering love you have shown me throughout my life, and for the boundless affection I receive every single day without fail.

To my father, Thys, who took me through an electrical course the very day I came out to him as gay! I anticipated chaos and turmoil, but he calmly responded with wisdom, saying, "Son, it's like a trip switch. Just reset all the breakers and flip the switch back on again... if it trips again, let's talk."

 And, of course, it tripped again! Thank you, Dad, for those Wednesday afternoon trips from Douglas to Wolmaransstad to see a therapist. It's safe to say that those sessions didn't yield much help either. At that time, they evaluated you on a scale of 1 to 10, and the rest, as they say, is history.

Years later, my dad approached me with an unforgettable and heartfelt offer: "Son, your mother and I want you to be genuinely happy. Be with someone who truly makes you happy!" And I did, indeed, find that happiness, which has been a beautiful journey.

To Andrew, who taught me from a young age that there are no such things as gay rights—thank you for that important lesson! Today, I fully understand that it's indeed true. There's no need to fight tirelessly for the basic right to simply be yourself and embrace who you are!

To Paul who trough the years safe me from myself at times and for a friendship that takes of where we left it every time.

Thank you, Laaitie, for instilling in me the belief to never give up on love, no matter the obstacles that stand in the way! To Johann and all the brave soldiers out there fighting this ongoing battle for acceptance and equality, I salute you with immense respect and admiration!

And lastly, to all those who cherish and uphold God's word, thank you for guiding me in learning to study the Scriptures on my own and fostering a deeper, more meaningful connection with my faith, which has enriched my life in countless ways.

To all the Girls... you help shaped me into the man I am today!

Contents

Chapter 1: Understanding Power Dynamics in the Gay Community

The Concept of Top and Bottom

The concept of "top" and "bottom" within the gay community often extends far beyond the simplistic notion of mere sexual roles, encompassing a much broader spectrum of identity, power dynamics, and interpersonal relationships. For many individuals within the gay community, these labels can carry a significant amount of weight, profoundly influencing not only how they perceive themselves but also how they are perceived by others in social contexts. The binary classification of these roles can create an environment laden with expectations and pressures, where individuals may feel an obligation to conform to specific roles based on various factors, including their personality traits, physical appearance, or age. This societal perspective can lead to a limited and narrow understanding of identity, ultimately constraining personal expression and authenticity, thereby inhibiting individuals from fully exploring and embracing their true selves.

Growing up, many gay individuals face an overwhelming barrage of perceptions from both within and outside the gay community. Young gay individuals often feel intense pressure to conform to societal archetypes of being a "top" or a "bottom," which are frequently dictated by stereotypes that associate certain personality traits and behaviours with these roles. For instance, those who are perceived as more feminine may be pushed toward the bottom role, while those who exhibit more masculine traits are often expected to take on the top role. This societal pressure can create a profound sense of dissonance for those who do not naturally align with these stereotypes, leading to internalized homophobia, feelings of inadequacy, and a struggle with self-identity. The societal call to "be yourself" can feel profoundly contradictory when societal norms impose such rigid and limiting expectations. This dissonance can further complicate the journey of self-acceptance for many young gay individuals.

Ageism also plays a critical and multifaceted role in how these dynamics unfold within the community. Younger individuals often encounter significant challenges when it comes to being taken seriously or feeling validated in their sexual identities. They are frequently viewed as inexperienced or too naïve to fully comprehend their roles within the broader social context. This perception can undermine their confidence and sense of belonging. Conversely, older gay men might face their own set of deeply ingrained stereotypes, where they are seen as out of touch with contemporary issues or, worse, deemed less desirable in a society that places a premium on youth. This pervasive age-related discrimination can lead to substantial mental health challenges, as individuals grapple with feelings of isolation and struggle to find their place in a community that often values youth and vitality over the invaluable experience and wisdom that come with age. The intersection of age and role can create further divisions that complicate the search for belonging and acceptance, making it even more difficult for individuals at both ends of the age spectrum to connect meaningfully with one another.

Authenticity versus expectation remains a central theme in navigating these complex identities. Many individuals grapple with the challenging balance of being true to themselves while feeling compelled to adhere to community norms that dictate specific behaviours or appearances. The pressure to conform can be incredibly overwhelming, often leading to significant mental health challenges such as anxiety and depression. Internalized homophobia can further exacerbate these feelings, as individuals may find themselves rejecting parts of their identity that do not fit the mold of what is considered acceptable within the community. It is absolutely crucial to acknowledge that these pressures can have profoundly detrimental effects on relationships, both romantic and platonic. This fosters an environment where acceptance is conditional, creating barriers to genuine connections and emotional well-being.

Understanding these dynamics is essential for promoting healthier interactions and supporting individuals in their journey toward self-acceptance.

To build truly supportive spaces for all members of the gay community, it is absolutely essential to actively challenge these societal norms and foster a deeper sense of inclusivity. Encouraging open and honest dialogue about the complexities of identity can play a significant role in dismantling the harmful stereotypes that are often associated with being a top or bottom. By creating environments that not only celebrate but also embrace diversity in age, appearance, gender identity, and expression, we can empower individuals to embrace their authentic selves without the pervasive fear of judgment or rejection. Additionally, by recognizing and addressing the profound impact of societal expectations on mental health and interpersonal relationships, families, friends, and community members can come together to cultivate a more accepting and supportive landscape for everyone. This collaborative effort allows every gay person to navigate their unique identity free from the constraints of rigid dichotomies, ultimately fostering a community where all can thrive and feel valued.

Historical Context of Power in Sexual Roles

The historical context of power in sexual roles within the gay community reveals a remarkably complex interplay of societal expectations, deeply ingrained internalized beliefs, and the ongoing evolution of individual and collective identity. Throughout various periods in history, the categorization of individuals based on sexual roles has frequently been influenced by both external perceptions and intricate internal dynamics. For many gay individuals, the pressure to conform to specific roles, often designated as "top" or "bottom," has roots in long-standing cultural stereotypes that shape and define notions of masculinity and femininity. These roles extend beyond mere personal preferences; they carry significant weight within the community, effectively shaping interpersonal relationships and establishing social hierarchies. Consequently, the expectations placed on individuals can lead to profound feelings of inadequacy and self-doubt, particularly among those who do not fit neatly into these rigid categories. This struggle for acceptance and identity reflects broader societal challenges, highlighting the need for a more nuanced understanding of sexual roles and their implications within the gay community.

The development of these sexual roles can be traced back to traditional views on masculinity and power. In many cultures, being a "top" has been associated with dominance, control, and traditional male attributes, while being a "bottom" has been linked to submission and vulnerability. This binary perspective can create significant pressure for individuals to embody certain traits, often leading to feelings of shame or inadequacy if they do not conform. The historical marginalization of gay identities has fuelled a reactionary need for individuals to assert their power through sexual roles, often at the expense of genuine self-expression. The result is a community grappling with the tension between authenticity and societal expectations.

Navigating these complex dynamics becomes even more challenging when considering the significant factors of age and appearance. Ageism within gay spaces not only complicates the power dynamics but also fosters a troubling hierarchy that is heavily based on youthfulness and physical attractiveness. Younger individuals may feel an intense pressure to adhere to specific stereotypes and behaviours in order to gain acceptance and validation from their peers, while older individuals often face the difficulty of being overlooked, dismissed, or even marginalized simply because of their age. This unfortunate situation creates an environment where both younger and older members of the gay community encounter unique challenges, often feeling excluded from spaces that are designed to offer support, understanding, and camaraderie. The pressure to conform to a narrow set of expectations regarding appearance and age can significantly exacerbate feelings of isolation and internalized homophobia. These experiences can ultimately lead to detrimental mental health outcomes, creating a cycle of distress that can be hard to escape.

The internalized homophobia that many individuals face is often compounded by the judgments based on appearance that persist within the gay community. The intense emphasis placed on physical looks can significantly dictate social standings and deeply influence relationships, leading to a culture where superficial attributes consistently overshadow genuine personality traits and the richness of individual character. This unhealthy focus on appearance reinforces harmful stereotypes that dictate who can be deemed a "top" or a "bottom," further entrenching complex power dynamics that can be difficult to navigate. As individuals strive to understand and express their identities, the pervasive fear of being judged solely based on looks can severely inhibit their ability to express their true selves and embrace their uniqueness. Consequently, many may feel trapped in roles that do not reflect their authentic desires or aspirations, perpetuating a cycle of conformity, dissatisfaction, and discontent that can be challenging to break free from.

Creating supportive and inclusive environments within the gay community is not just important but essential for dismantling the deeply rooted and harmful power dynamics that have persisted over time. By acknowledging and embracing the diverse experiences and identities that exist within the community, we pave the way for a broader and more nuanced understanding of what it truly means to be gay. Emphasizing acceptance and actively encouraging authentic self-expression can significantly help alleviate the pressures and burdens that come with stereotypes and predefined roles. By fostering safe spaces where individuals feel empowered to explore their identities without the fear of judgment or rejection, the community can make significant strides toward a more inclusive future that genuinely values and celebrates each person's unique contributions. Ultimately, addressing the historical context of power dynamics in sexual roles is not merely beneficial but crucial for empowering all individuals within the gay spectrum to live authentically and without any imposed constraints or limitations.

The Evolution of Gay Identity

The evolution of gay identity represents a profoundly intricate journey, intricately marked by significant societal changes, deeply personal struggles, and the ongoing negotiation of one's sense of self within a rich and diverse community. Historically, being gay was frequently enveloped in secrecy and deep-seated shame, with prevailing societal norms dictating rigid gender roles and expectations that often marginalized those who identified as gay. As gay individuals began to emerge from the shadows of societal oppression, they faced a myriad of complex challenges, including the critical need for acceptance from family, friends, and the larger society, in addition to grappling with their own internal conflicts regarding their sexual identity and orientation. This evolution is characterized not only by the relentless quest for acceptance but also by the courageous fight against the pervasive stereotypes and misconceptions that have long permeated the community and contributed to discrimination and misunderstanding. Through perseverance and resilience, the journey continues to unfold, reflecting the ongoing struggle for recognition and equality.

Navigating identity within the gay community can often feel like walking a precarious tightrope, balancing the quest for authenticity against the significant pressures of societal expectations. Many individuals find themselves confronting a variety of stereotypes, particularly those associated with their prescribed roles as tops or bottoms, which can lead to profound feelings of inadequacy or a deep disconnection from their true selves. The pervasive notion of being "too old" or "too young," along with the judgments placed on masculinity or femininity, can create substantial barriers to genuine self-acceptance and personal growth. In a vibrant community that purports to champion individuality and self-expression, the paradox of conformity can be, especially disheartening. Members often grapple with the ongoing desire to fully embrace who they are while simultaneously seeking validation and acceptance from others, which can lead to internal conflicts and emotional turmoil. This intricate dance between self-identity and societal pressure continues to shape the experiences and challenges faced by individuals within the community.

Ageism within gay spaces creates additional complexities in the landscape of gay identity. Young gay individuals often feel dismissed, overlooked, or even patronized, while older members frequently encounter marginalization or face assumptions regarding their relevance in contemporary discussions. This generational divide can result in a significant lack of mentorship and understanding, making it increasingly difficult for individuals across age groups to navigate their identities effectively. The challenges encountered by both younger and older members of the gay community serve to highlight the critical importance of fostering intergenerational dialogue and support. Such connections are essential for cultivating a cohesive and vibrant community where all voices are heard and valued, ultimately leading to greater understanding and solidarity among its members.

Internalized homophobia continues to be a significant and detrimental barrier to the development of healthy, fulfilling relationships within the gay community. The pervasive impact of societal stigma can manifest deeply in feelings of self-doubt and negative self-perception, leading individuals to grapple with their sense of worth, attractiveness, and overall desirability. Such internal conflicts can severely exacerbate the challenges associated with forming meaningful and lasting connections, as individuals may inadvertently project their insecurities onto partners or peers, creating misunderstandings and emotional distance. Recognizing and addressing these deeply rooted issues is absolutely crucial for promoting mental well-being and fostering a more inclusive environment where everyone feels valued, respected, and accepted for who they truly are. Through collective awareness and support, we can work towards breaking down these barriers and nurturing healthier relationships within the community.

Creating supportive spaces for all members of the gay community is absolutely vital for fostering a genuine sense of belonging and acceptance among individuals. As the complex dynamics of power between tops and bottoms continue to influence social interactions within the community, it becomes increasingly important to actively challenge the stereotypes that dictate and often limit these roles. By building inclusive environments where diverse expressions of identity are celebrated and embraced, we can help alleviate the significant pressures faced by individuals, thereby allowing them to fully embrace their authentic selves without fear of judgment or rejection from others. Furthermore, by prioritizing mental health and nurturing meaningful community connections, the ongoing evolution of gay identity can progress toward a future that not only values diversity but also champions self-expression in all its forms. This commitment to inclusivity will ultimately strengthen the community as a whole, creating a richer tapestry of experiences and identities.

Chapter 2: Growing Up Gay: Perceptions and Realities

Coming Out: A Universal Experience

Coming out is a deeply personal and transformative journey that resonates universally across the diverse spectrum of gay experiences. For many individuals, it marks a significant turning point in their lives, often filled with a mix of anticipation, hope, and trepidation. While the act of revealing one's sexual orientation can be profoundly liberating and empowering, it simultaneously exposes individuals to the complexities of societal expectations, internal pressures, and the varied reactions of those around them. The narrative surrounding coming out is frequently framed by the struggles faced during formative years, where perceptions and attitudes are shaped not only by family and peers but also by the broader gay community and societal norms. This experience is rarely linear; it is often characterized by moments of acceptance and joy juxtaposed with the harsh realities of judgment, misunderstanding, and potential rejection. Each person's journey is unique, marked by personal revelations and the quest for authenticity in an often unaccepting world.

The pressure to conform to specific stereotypes within the gay community can significantly complicate the already challenging coming out process. Many individuals find themselves grappling with the complex idea of what it truly means to be "gay enough" or fitting into predefined categories such as "top" or "bottom." These often rigid labels can create a narrow and limiting understanding of identity, leading to deep feelings of inadequacy and self-doubt among those who don't neatly align with these societal expectations. The pervasive notion that one must embody a certain type of gay identity, whether perceived as being too feminine or too masculine, can further hinder one's acceptance and sense of belonging within the community. This adds to the emotional labour involved in the coming out journey, creating a paradox where the very space that is meant to provide support can, in some instances, perpetuate exclusion and judgment, making the experience even more difficult for individuals navigating their authentic selves.

Ageism complicates the dynamics of the gay community in significant ways, presenting unique and multifaceted challenges for both younger and older individuals. Younger gay individuals may face scrutiny not only for their perceived lack of experience but also for their youthful exuberance and energy, which can sometimes be misunderstood or dismissed by others. On the other hand, older members of the community often struggle to find relevance and a sense of belonging in a space that tends to prioritize youth and vitality, leaving them feeling overlooked. This situation creates a scenario where each group can feel marginalized and isolated, contributing to a disconnect that diminishes the overall sense of community and shared experience. The complex interplay between age and identity can intensify feelings of loneliness and exclusion, making it essential for families, friends, and allies to understand these nuances. Such understanding is crucial as they support their loved ones through the often challenging process of coming out and navigating their identities within the community.

Authenticity emerges as a crucial theme in the lives of many gay individuals as they navigate the complex landscape of their identities against the often rigid backdrop of community norms and societal expectations. The immense pressure to conform to these expectations can lead to internalized homophobia, where deep-seated self-hatred manifests as a direct result of pervasive societal stigmas and discrimination. This internal conflict can have a profound impact on relationships, frequently resulting in significant difficulties in forming and maintaining healthy, meaningful connections with others. The ongoing struggle between being true to oneself and adhering to external pressures can create a detrimental cycle of self-doubt and insecurity, reinforcing the urgent need for supportive environments that genuinely encourage authenticity and self-acceptance without fear of judgment or reprisal.

Creating inclusive and supportive spaces is absolutely essential for fostering a genuine sense of belonging among all individuals within the vast gay spectrum. By actively engaging in efforts to dismantle the harmful stereotypes and age-related barriers that frequently plague the community, families, friends, and allies can play a crucial role in shaping a more accepting and understanding culture. Encouraging and facilitating open dialogue about identity, alongside the varied and often complex experiences of coming out, can significantly help mitigate the mental health challenges faced by many gay youths. This vital support not only empowers individuals to embrace their authentic selves with confidence but also strengthens the deep ties that bind families and communities together. Ultimately, this leads to a richer, more nuanced, and diverse understanding of what it truly means to be part of the gay experience, fostering a culture of acceptance, love, and unity that benefits everyone involved.

The Influence of Peers and Society

The influence of peers and society plays an undeniably crucial role in shaping the experiences of gay individuals, often creating a complex and intricate web of expectations that can be incredibly difficult to navigate. As young gay individuals come to terms with their identities, they are frequently bombarded with a myriad of perceptions and stereotypes from both within the gay community and the larger, more mainstream society. This multifaceted phenomenon can lead to deep feelings of inadequacy, particularly when individuals feel they do not conform to the narrow, often rigid definitions of what it means to be gay. The pressure to fit into a specific mold—whether that mold is based on age, femininity or masculinity, or particular sexual roles— can create significant internal conflict and substantially hinder one's journey toward genuine self-acceptance. This struggle is compounded by the fear of judgment and rejection from both peers and society, making the path to embracing one's true self even more challenging.

In the gay community, the idea of being true to oneself is frequently celebrated as a fundamental guiding principle. However, the reality of this expectation can be far more complex and nuanced. Many individuals within the community grapple with pervasive stereotypes that dictate how they should look, behave, or even express their sexuality. For instance, there exists a prevailing belief that one must be "masculine enough" to assume the role of a top or "feminine enough" to take on the role of a bottom. This kind of rigid categorization can lead to internalized homophobia and deep-seated feelings of shame. Such societal pressures can be particularly damaging during formative years, as young gay individuals often feel an intense compulsion to suppress their true selves in order to achieve acceptance from their peers and the broader community. The struggle to navigate these often conflicting expectations can result in significant mental health challenges, as the heavy burden of community norms collides with personal identity, creating a tumultuous internal landscape that can be difficult to manage.

Ageism presents a significant and complex challenge in gay spaces, where both younger and older members may often feel marginalized and overlooked. Younger individuals in the gay community may experience feelings of invisibility or condescension from older community members, who may not fully grasp or appreciate their unique experiences and perspectives. Conversely, older members of the gay community may feel increasingly alienated by the rapid evolution of cultural norms, trends, and expectations, which can lead to a profound sense of disconnect from the younger generations. This generational divide not only fosters feelings of isolation but also reinforces the notion that there is a singular, standardized way to be gay, ultimately neglecting and undermining the rich tapestry of diverse experiences and identities that exist within the community. Embracing this diversity is essential for fostering a more inclusive and supportive environment for all.

The dynamics of power within the gay community, particularly concerning the top versus bottom narrative, significantly complicate the quest for authenticity and self-identity. These roles come with their own intricate sets of stereotypes and societal expectations that can greatly dictate how individuals relate to one another on both emotional and physical levels. The pressure to conform to a certain role can create substantial tension and conflict in relationships, as partners navigate their own desires while trying to meet the often rigid societal expectations placed upon them. This complex dynamic can also extend its influence on friendships, as individuals may feel a strong compulsion to align themselves with specific groups based on their perceived roles within the community, often leading to feelings of isolation or exclusion. The ongoing struggle for authenticity amidst these overwhelming pressures can result in a fractured sense of self, where individuals may feel they cannot fully express who they truly are or what they genuinely desire, leading to internal conflict and dissatisfaction.

Building supportive spaces is absolutely critical for fostering an inclusive environment where all members of the gay community can truly thrive and flourish. Families, friends, and peers play an incredibly vital role in creating these nurturing spaces, as they possess the unique power to challenge deep-rooted stereotypes and promote a culture of acceptance and understanding. Encouraging open and honest dialogue about the rich and diverse expressions of gay identity can significantly help dismantle the harmful expectations and pressures that many individuals face in their daily lives. By fostering an atmosphere of understanding, compassion, and unwavering support, loved ones can empower gay individuals to fully embrace their authentic selves, liberating them from the burdens of societal and communal pressures that often weigh heavily on them. This profound sense of belonging is essential for mental well-being and can ultimately lead to healthier, more fulfilling relationships within the community, allowing everyone to connect on a deeper level and support one another in their journeys.

Navigating Youth and Sexuality

Navigating youth and sexuality is an intricate and multifaceted journey that involves not only personal discovery but also the significant influence of societal pressures and community expectations. For young gay individuals, the process of understanding and embracing their sexual identity can be further complicated by the perceptions and attitudes held by others within the gay community. Many find themselves grappling with labels that dictate how they should express their sexuality, which can be an overwhelming experience. This often leads to feelings of inadequacy, confusion, or frustration when they don't fit neatly into the predefined boxes of "top" or "bottom," "masculine" or "feminine." These rigid categorizations can create a profound sense of isolation, as those who do not conform to these expectations may feel rejected, marginalized, or completely misunderstood, even within spaces and communities that are supposed to be welcoming and inclusive to all. Such challenges can hinder their ability to fully explore and express their true selves, contributing to a broader struggle for acceptance and belonging.

The dynamics within the gay community frequently mirror broader societal norms, including the issue of ageism, which can lead to the marginalization of both younger and older members. Younger individuals often grapple with being perceived as overly inexperienced or immature, while older individuals may experience feelings of exclusion, as the community tends to celebrate youth and vitality more prominently. This tension related to age can create an environment where individuals on both ends of the age spectrum feel pressured to conform to specific ideals and standards, making it increasingly challenging for them to authentically express their true selves. The deep-seated desire to belong to a community can compel many to adhere to these stereotypes, sometimes resulting in the suppression of their genuine identities in Favor of fitting in with perceived norms.

Authenticity is an essential and fundamental aspect of successfully navigating one's sexuality, yet the pressure to conform to community expectations can often feel overwhelming and stifling. Many young gay individuals encounter a range of conflicting messages about how to present themselves— struggling to balance the encouragement to "be yourself" with the pervasive fear of being judged harshly for not fitting neatly into established norms and stereotypes. This ongoing tension can lead to internalized homophobia, where individuals absorb and internalize negative societal attitudes toward same-gender attraction, which can severely affect their self-worth, confidence, and the quality of their relationships. When individuals feel they must suppress their true selves in a desperate bid for acceptance and approval, the consequences for their mental health can be profoundly detrimental. This struggle may manifest as heightened anxiety, deep-seated depression, or a pervasive sense of disconnection from both their authentic selves and their peers, leaving them feeling isolated and misunderstood in a society that often demands conformity.

'Appearance plays an undeniably significant role in the judgments faced by gay youth. The intense emphasis on physical looks and the relentless pressure to adhere to specific aesthetic standards can create a superficial hierarchy within the community that many feel they must navigate. Young people may feel compelled to alter their appearance in various ways to be deemed attractive or acceptable by their peers, which often leads to an ongoing cycle of comparison and deep-seated self-doubt. This overwhelming focus on looks can overshadow and diminish the appreciation for deeper qualities, such as kindness, intellect, and emotional depth, which are essential for forming and nurturing meaningful relationships. As a result, many young individuals struggle profoundly to find genuine connections, feeling trapped in a culture that frequently prioritizes surface over substance, leaving them longing for authentic interactions that truly reflect who they are beyond mere appearances.'

Creating supportive spaces is absolutely essential for fostering genuine authenticity and deep acceptance within the gay community. Families, friends, and allies play a pivotal and indispensable role in providing safe environments where young individuals can freely explore their identities without the constant fear of judgment or rejection. By encouraging open dialogues about sexuality, actively challenging harmful stereotypes, and joyfully celebrating the incredible diversity within the community, we can work to dismantle the oppressive structures that often dictate behaviour and identity. By prioritizing inclusivity, compassion, and understanding, we can empower gay youth to confidently embrace their true selves, liberated from the weight of societal expectations and the limitations imposed by internalized biases. This supportive framework not only benefits individuals but significantly strengthens the community as a whole, allowing for a richer tapestry of experiences, identities, and stories to flourish, ultimately leading to a more vibrant and cohesive community.

Chapter 3: Stereotypes and Their Impact

The Pressure of Conformity

The pressure of conformity within the gay community represents a complex and multifaceted dynamic that can significantly impact individuals' self-perception, emotional well-being, and overall mental health. As gay individuals navigate their unique identities, they frequently encounter societal expectations that dictate not only how they should look and act but also how they should relate to others in various social contexts. This pressure is exacerbated by pervasive stereotypes that categorize members of the community into rigid and often simplistic roles, such as 'tops' and 'bottoms,' which can lead to deep feelings of inadequacy and self-doubt among those who do not fit neatly into these predefined boxes. The challenge of conforming to these stereotypes can be particularly pronounced for individuals who are perceived as either too feminine or too masculine, resulting in internalized homophobia that complicates their journey toward self-acceptance and self-love. As they grapple with these external pressures and internal conflicts, the struggle for authenticity becomes increasingly difficult, highlighting the need for greater understanding and acceptance within the community itself.

Ageism plays a notably significant role in the pressure to conform within gay spaces, impacting how individuals of different ages perceive themselves and their place within the community. Young individuals often feel compelled to adopt behaviours or attitudes that seem more aligned with being older or more seasoned than their actual age suggests, which can lead to a sense of inauthenticity. Conversely, older individuals may experience marginalization and exclusion based on their age, leading to a perception that their contributions are undervalued. This creates a complex dichotomy in which younger members might feel they lack the wisdom or experience necessary to effectively navigate community norms, while older members may struggle with being sidelined or ignored in discussions about identity, belonging, and the evolution of the community. The intersection of age and identity can generate profound feelings of isolation and disconnect among individuals, making it imperative for the community to actively foster an inclusive environment where individuals of all ages are genuinely valued, respected, and given equal opportunities to contribute to conversations and activities.

Authenticity versus expectation is an essential theme in the ongoing conversation about conformity within the gay community. Many advocates emphasize the importance of being true to oneself and embracing one's unique identity; however, the reality often reveals a stark and troubling contrast. Individuals may find themselves caught in a complex struggle, torn between their true selves and the various personas they feel pressured to adopt to gain acceptance and approval from their peers. This internal conflict for authenticity can lead to significant mental health challenges, as the weight of community expectations can feel utterly overwhelming at times. The pressure to perform a particular identity can gradually erode self-esteem and exacerbate feelings of loneliness and isolation, particularly for those who feel they do not align with the popular and often narrow representations of gay identities that dominate societal discourse. This ongoing struggle highlights the need for a more inclusive understanding of identity within the community.

Appearance and societal judgments based on looks add further layers of complexity to the already significant pressure of conformity. Within the gay community, there is often an elevated emphasis placed on physical appearance, which can create an environment where individuals feel a compelling need to conform to specific and sometimes unrealistic beauty standards in order to gain acceptance. This situation can foster a vicious cycle in which those who do not fit the idealized image may experience feelings of marginalization, ultimately impacting their relationships, self-esteem, and overall sense of belonging within the community. The intense obsession with appearance can easily overshadow the diverse and multifaceted qualities that contribute to a person's true identity, making it increasingly difficult for individuals to appreciate and celebrate their unique attributes without constantly viewing themselves through the critical lens of comparison to others.

Building supportive spaces that prioritize inclusivity is absolutely essential in alleviating the immense pressures of conformity that often exist within the gay community. By creating environments where all identities are not just acknowledged but genuinely embraced, we foster a profound sense of belonging that significantly reduces the stigma associated with not conforming to typical stereotypes. It is vital for family members, friends, and allies to fully understand and actively advocate for the rich diversity that exists within the gay spectrum. This advocacy encourages individuals to express their true selves freely, without the persistent fear of judgment or rejection. By consistently challenging the stereotypes and entrenched power dynamics that perpetuate these pressures, the community can collectively move towards a much more inclusive future. In such a future, every individual feels valued, respected, and supported in their unique journey of self-discovery, allowing for a vibrant tapestry of identities to thrive.

Misconceptions of Masculinity and Femininity

Misconceptions surrounding masculinity and femininity play a significant and profound role in shaping the experiences of gay individuals within their diverse communities. These misconceptions often manifest in rigid and limiting stereotypes that dictate how one should behave based solely on their sexual orientation. For many individuals, there exists a prevailing and deeply ingrained belief that to be considered a "real" man, one must strictly adhere to traditional gender norms and expectations. This belief can create a hostile and unwelcoming environment for those who do not fit neatly into these narrow categories, leading to internalized homophobia, feelings of inadequacy, and a struggle for self-acceptance. As a result, many individuals grapple with the pressure to conform to societal standards, which can have a lasting impact on their mental health and overall well-being.

The pressure to conform to societal expectations can be particularly intense within the gay community itself, creating an environment where individuals often feel compelled to follow certain unwritten rules. Many individuals find themselves scrutinized not only by the heterosexual world but also by their peers within their own community. For example, the pervasive assumption that certain types of gay men must be either overly masculine or overly feminine can lead to exclusion and harsh judgment from others. Those who do not conform to these rigid stereotypes may be labelled as "too fem to be a top" or "too masculine to be a bottom," which can be incredibly damaging to their self-esteem and deeply affect their sense of identity. This internal scrutiny adds another layer of complexity to the already challenging dynamics of self-acceptance and belonging within the community.

Ageism further complicates the intricate landscape of gay identity, as both younger and older individuals encounter a variety of unique challenges that are often overlooked. Young gay individuals may struggle significantly with being taken seriously within their own community, facing scepticism about their experiences and perspectives. Meanwhile, older gay individuals often grapple with the pervasive notion that they have somehow become less relevant or desirable within the community, leading to feelings of invisibility. This age-related bias not only adversely affects personal relationships but also deeply influences the dynamics of power, attraction, and social interaction. The intersection of age and entrenched stereotypes can create an environment where individuals feel an intense pressure to perform a version of masculinity or femininity that may not truly align with their authentic selves, ultimately stifling their personal expression and well-being.

Navigating the expectations of authenticity versus societal norms can be particularly taxing and emotionally draining. Many individuals within the gay community strive to be true to themselves while simultaneously feeling the heavy weight of community expectations pressing down on them. The ideal of being "yourself" often clashes with the harsh reality of judgment based on superficial aspects such as appearance or behaviour. This ongoing tension can lead to significant mental health challenges, as individuals grapple deeply with the desire for acceptance against the often overwhelming backdrop of imposed stereotypes. The fear of not fitting in can prevent many from fully exploring their identities and expressing their true selves, further complicating their journey toward self-acceptance and fulfilment.

To foster a more inclusive and welcoming environment, it is absolutely essential to actively challenge and confront these prevalent misconceptions of masculinity and femininity that exist within the gay community. Building supportive and nurturing spaces that genuinely embrace a wide range of diversity in expression and identity can significantly help alleviate the pressure that individuals feel to conform to harmful and limiting stereotypes. By encouraging open and constructive dialogue about the complexities of identity, the effects of ageism, and the profound impact of internalized homophobia, we can empower individuals to break free from the constraints imposed by society. Ultimately, recognizing, addressing, and dismantling these misconceptions will create an environment where all members of the gay community can thrive authentically, express themselves freely, and live without fear of judgment or rejection.

The Danger of Typecasting

The concept of typecasting within the gay community presents significant challenges for individuals as they navigate their complex identities. Being labelled as a specific "type" can severely restrict personal expression and create substantial barriers to authentic self-representation. The pressure to conform to particular stereotypes—such as being perceived as too masculine or too feminine for designated roles—can lead to deep feelings of inadequacy and internal conflict. This phenomenon is especially pronounced among younger members of the gay community, who often feel compelled to fit into predefined molds that may not resonate with their true and authentic selves. The societal pressure to adhere to these expectations can significantly hinder personal growth and exploration of one's identity, making it even more difficult for individuals to embrace their uniqueness and develop a genuine sense of self. Such challenges can create an environment where self-acceptance is overshadowed by the need for external validation, ultimately affecting mental well-being and the ability to form meaningful connections.

In many cases, internalized homophobia significantly exacerbates the negative effects of typecasting. When gay individuals internalize the harmful negative perceptions and pervasive stereotypes surrounding their sexual orientation, they may judge themselves harshly against the often unrealistic and restrictive standards set by both the broader society and their peers. This intense self-criticism can lead to various mental health challenges, such as heightened anxiety, deep-seated depression, and a constant sense of inadequacy, as individuals struggle to reconcile their true selves with the rigid identities imposed upon them by external pressures. The stigma associated with being perceived as "not gay enough" or "too gay" creates a toxic and unwelcoming environment, where individuals feel an overwhelming compulsion to hide their authentic selves in order to gain acceptance and validation within both the larger community and their own social circles.

Ageism significantly influences the dynamics of typecasting within the gay community. Older gay individuals frequently encounter challenges related to invisibility and marginalization, often feeling overlooked or excluded from conversations and spaces that prioritize youth. Conversely, younger members may struggle with being dismissed as inexperienced or naïve, facing scepticism about their perspectives and contributions. This tension between these distinct age groups frequently leads to a pronounced lack of understanding and support, which only serves to reinforce harmful stereotypes that pit one generation against another. Such a generational divide complicates the quest for acceptance and belonging, as both younger and older individuals must navigate a complex landscape shaped by differing societal expectations, experiences, and values that can hinder unity and mutual respect within the community.

The impact of appearance significantly complicates the issue of typecasting within the gay community. Judgments based on superficial looks can lead to hasty and often misguided assessments of individuals, which frequently overshadow their unique qualities, experiences, and the rich depth of their personalities. This persistent fixation on physical attributes can create a challenging environment where self-worth becomes inextricably linked to external validation and societal standards. Consequently, individuals who do not fit conventional ideals of attractiveness may struggle to feel valued and accepted within their own community. This damaging cycle of judgment can perpetuate deep-seated feelings of inadequacy and insecurity, ultimately pushing individuals further away from embracing their true identities and reinforcing harmful stereotypes that do not reflect the diverse realities of the community.

Creating supportive spaces for all members of the gay community is not just essential, but imperative in combating the dangers of typecasting that can limit personal expression. By actively fostering an environment that not only celebrates diversity but also encourages authenticity and individuality, individuals can feel truly empowered to express themselves freely without the often heavy constraints imposed by societal expectations. It is crucial for allies—friends, family, and community members alike—to take a stand and actively challenge stereotypes while promoting a culture of acceptance and understanding. By recognizing the intricate and complex interplay of identity, age, appearance, and the various societal pressures that individuals face, we can collectively work together to build a more inclusive community that honours and respects the individuality of each person. This inclusive approach allows everyone to thrive in a safe space, free from the fear of judgment or rejection, ensuring that all voices are heard and valued.

Chapter 4: Ageism in Gay Spaces

Challenges Faced by Younger Gays

Younger gay individuals frequently navigate a complex and often challenging environment shaped by societal norms, peer attitudes, and deeply rooted beliefs regarding their identities. While growing up in a more accepting world can certainly be beneficial, it does not entirely eliminate the significant difficulties that arise when exploring one's identity amid conflicting messages. Many young gay people experience a profound contradiction where they are encouraged to be true to themselves yet simultaneously face judgment based on their sexual orientation and the expectations imposed upon them by their families and the broader community. This unique pressure leads to a distinct array of challenges that can deeply impact their self-esteem, mental well-being, and overall sense of belonging in a world that sometimes feels unwelcoming. The struggle to reconcile these conflicting experiences can create a turbulent emotional landscape, influencing their relationships and personal growth as they seek to define who they are in a society that often sends mixed signals.

One of the notable pressures comes from the expectations within the gay community itself, which can be quite pronounced. Many young gay individuals feel a strong compulsion to conform to specific stereotypes, such as being more masculine or feminine, which can be both limiting and exclusionary in nature. This societal pressure creates a situation where those who do not fit neatly into these conventional categories may experience feelings of alienation or marginalization. The pervasive notion that one must adhere to a particular type of masculinity or femininity to be accepted as a top or a bottom can further complicate their self-image and lead to deep-seated feelings of inadequacy. Such pressures can leave young individuals grappling with questions about their worth and identity, contributing to an ongoing struggle for acceptance and validation, both within the community and in broader society. This complex dynamic underscore the challenges faced by many as they navigate their personal journeys of self-discovery and belonging.

Ageism also plays a significant role in the multitude of challenges faced by younger members of the gay community. The community is often characterized by a pronounced generational divide, where the voices and experiences of older individuals may overshadow those of younger members. This dynamic can lead to a profound sense of disconnect, as younger gay people may find that their unique experiences and perspectives are often dismissed or undervalued by their older counterparts. The pervasive fear of being labelled as "too young" or "too inexperienced" can significantly hinder their ability to express themselves authentically and engage fully within community spaces. This tension related to age can foster an environment where younger individuals feel immense pressure to constantly prove themselves, often leading to challenges that can negatively impact their mental well-being and overall sense of belonging within the community.

Navigating the complex intersection of authenticity and community expectations can be particularly daunting for many individuals. Numerous younger members of the gay community grapple with the profound desire to express their true selves while simultaneously facing the harsh reality of how they are perceived by those around them. This conflict between the need to be true to oneself and the pressure to meet the often unrealistic expectations of peers can lead to the troubling phenomenon of internalized homophobia. In this scenario, individuals may internalize negative stereotypes and societal attitudes about their identities, which can be incredibly damaging. This internal struggle can manifest in various ways, including feelings of self-doubt, anxiety, and even depression. Therefore, it becomes essential for the community to create and maintain affirming spaces that not only celebrate diversity but also actively resist and reject restrictive norms that can stifle personal expression and authenticity.

Lastly, the focus on appearance within the gay community can significantly exacerbate these challenges. Judgments based on looks can create an environment where young gay people feel immense pressure to conform to idealized body types or fashion standards to gain acceptance from their peers. This strong emphasis on physical appearance can often overshadow the critical importance of personality, interests, and individuality, leading to an unhealthy fixation on image rather than authenticity. To build a genuinely supportive and inclusive environment for individuals of all sexual orientations, it is absolutely crucial for families, friends, and community members to actively challenge these stereotypes. By doing so, they can encourage young gay people to embrace their uniqueness and celebrate their true selves without the fear of judgment or rejection from others.

Experiences of Older Gays

Experiences of older gay individuals often illuminate the intricate complexities involved in navigating their identities within a community that, on one hand, fervently champions authenticity while, on the other hand, enforces rigid, sometimes limiting stereotypes. As they take the time to reflect on their diverse journeys, many older gay individuals recount the significant challenges they faced while growing up in an era characterized by vastly different societal norms and expectations. The pressure to conform to specific archetypes, such as adhering to a particular type of gay persona, frequently leads to profound feelings of inadequacy, alienation, and disconnection from one's true self. This dichotomy creates a unique and often challenging environment where individuals may grapple with feelings of being too old or too young, too feminine to be considered a top, or too masculine to fit the role of a bottom. This results in an ongoing struggle for self-acceptance that continues to persist, even amidst peers who share similar experiences and backgrounds.

Older gay people often confront significant ageism within various gay spaces, where the celebration of youth is frequently prioritized, leading to a sense of marginalization for older individuals. The prevalent perception that queer culture predominantly revolves around youth can foster a profound feeling of invisibility among older members of the community. This pervasive ageist attitude not only disrupts social dynamics but also profoundly impacts mental health, as older gay people struggle with feelings of exclusion and the pervasive fear of being perceived as irrelevant or outdated. The complex intersection of age and sexual identity presents unique and multifaceted challenges, compelling older individuals to assert their rightful place within a community that may not always acknowledge or appreciate their valuable contributions, experiences, and wisdom.

In the process of defining their identities, older gay individuals frequently confront a complex tension between authenticity and the expectations imposed by society. The well-known mantra of "be yourself" can become significantly complicated when community norms dictate particular behaviours, lifestyles, or appearances that individuals feel pressured to adopt. Many older individuals report feeling an intense pressure to conform and fit into established roles, which can ultimately stifle their true selves and inhibit self-expression. This internal conflict is further exacerbated by a strong desire for acceptance and belonging within the community, creating a challenging cycle where individuals may suppress their genuine identities in order to align with perceived norms. As a result, this struggle can lead to emotional distress and hinder their overall emotional well-being, making it increasingly difficult for them to navigate their identities in a way that feels true to themselves.

The impact of internalized homophobia represents another significant and complex aspect of the experiences faced by older gay individuals. Many of these individuals carry the heavy burden of societal stigma, which can lead to deeply rooted negative self-perceptions that adversely affect their relationships and interactions within the community. This internalized bias often manifests in various ways, influencing how they engage with others and creating substantial barriers to forming genuine connections. As they navigate their personal and social relationships, older gay individuals may frequently find themselves questioning their own worth or the validity of their lived experiences, which can perpetuate a sense of isolation and loneliness rather than fostering a sense of community solidarity and support among peers. This struggle with internalized homophobia can significantly hinder their ability to connect meaningfully with others, further complicating their journey towards acceptance and belonging within the broader gay community.

Finally, the dynamics of power within the gay community, particularly the top versus bottom narrative, significantly complicate the experiences of older individuals. These roles, which are often laden with deep social implications, come with a range of expectations that can be quite difficult to navigate, especially for those who do not fit neatly into these established categories. Judgments based on appearance and role can lead to the creation of a hierarchy that ultimately undermines the very essence of inclusivity that the community strives to uphold. To build truly supportive spaces, it is absolutely essential to actively challenge these pervasive stereotypes and to create welcoming environments where all individuals, regardless of age, identity, or sexual orientation, can feel genuinely valued and accepted. This collective effort can profoundly transform the landscape of the gay community, fostering a more inclusive culture that honours and respects the diverse experiences of older gay people while simultaneously acknowledging and embracing those of younger generations. By working together, we can cultivate a community that reflects the richness of all its members, ensuring that everyone has a place and a voice.

Bridging the Generation Gap

Bridging the generation gap within the gay community requires a nuanced and comprehensive understanding of the various pressures faced by individuals at different life stages. For many gay individuals, the journey of growing up comes with a unique set of challenges, which are shaped by both societal expectations and issues that arise from within the community itself. Younger members often grapple with stereotypes that dictate how they should express their identities, leading to profound feelings of inadequacy or alienation. For instance, the prevailing notion that one must conform to a specific archetype—whether it be perceived as too feminine to be a top or too masculine to be a bottom—can create significant internal conflict and perpetuate a destructive cycle of self-doubt. These pressures can exacerbate the mental health challenges faced by gay youth, who may already be dealing with external homophobia and discrimination, making their struggle for acceptance even more complex and painful.

Conversely, older generations within the gay community confront their own unique set of challenges, often arising from ageism and the prevailing perception that they do not align with the contemporary narratives of what it means to be gay today. They may find themselves marginalized or overlooked in spaces that predominantly celebrate and prioritize youth culture, which can lead to profound feelings of invisibility and exclusion. This disconnect can foster not only resentment but also misunderstanding between younger and older members of the gay community, as both groups grapple with their identities in a world that often seems to value certain experiences over others. Bridging this generational gap requires a concerted effort of empathy and open dialogue, creating opportunities for the sharing of rich stories that highlight the diverse and multifaceted journeys within the community, ultimately fostering greater understanding and connection among all ages.

The internalized homophobia that can arise from these complex dynamics significantly complicates relationships among gay individuals within the community. When members of the community cling to harmful stereotypes about age, appearance, or sexual roles, they can inadvertently perpetuate a culture rife with judgment and exclusion. This situation can create a toxic environment where individuals feel immense pressure to conform to narrow, often unrealistic definitions of what authenticity means. It is absolutely crucial to create and maintain supportive spaces that wholeheartedly embrace diversity in age, expression, and experience. Such inclusive environments not only validate and honour individual experiences but also foster collaboration and understanding across generational lines, ultimately strengthening the community as a whole. By doing so, we can cultivate a more unified and empathetic society that celebrates every individual's unique contribution.

Authenticity versus expectation remains a fundamental and ongoing theme in the discourse surrounding the gay community. Many individuals grapple with the challenge of reconciling their true selves with the often rigid and sometimes overwhelming expectations imposed by both societies at large and their peers. This tension becomes particularly pronounced in discussions regarding sexual roles, where the binary classification of top and bottom can frequently overshadow the inherent complexity and diversity of human sexuality. Encouraging open and honest conversations about these multifaceted topics can significantly contribute to dismantling harmful stereotypes and fostering a more inclusive narrative that genuinely honours the rich spectrum of identities present within the community. By actively embracing a more fluid understanding of roles, expressions, and experiences, individuals can discover empowerment in fully embracing their authentic selves, ultimately leading to a deeper sense of self-acceptance, and belonging.

Ultimately, bridging the generation gap within the community requires a steadfast commitment to building inclusive environments where all voices are not only heard but also genuinely valued. This process involves recognizing and understanding the unique challenges faced by both younger and older members of the gay community while actively working to support and uplift one another. By fostering meaningful intergenerational connections and conversations, the community can create a more cohesive and supportive atmosphere that effectively counters the pressures of harmful stereotypes and societal expectations. This thoughtful approach not only enriches the individual experiences of community members but also significantly strengthens the community as a whole, paving the way for a more united, empowered, and resilient future that celebrates diversity in all its forms.

Chapter 5: Authenticity vs. Expectation

The Struggle for Self-Expression

The journey of self-expression for many gay individuals is often fraught with a multitude of challenges, significantly influenced by deeply ingrained societal perceptions and the weight of community expectations. Growing up, many face an intense internal struggle that is compounded by relentless external judgments from peers and society at large. For some, the immense pressure to conform to specific stereotypes becomes overwhelmingly burdensome. These stereotypes often dictate who can assume particular roles in relationships, such as the dominant "top" or submissive "bottom," creating rigid expectations. This dynamic can lead to profound internal conflict, where individuals feel compelled to fit into predefined molds that do not resonate with their true identities, ultimately undermining their authentic selves. The irony lies in a community that fervently advocates for self-acceptance and personal freedom yet imposes stringent norms that can feel exclusionary and restrictive, leaving many feelings isolated in their quest for genuine expression.

Navigating identity within the gay community encompasses not just personal discovery but also the challenge of confronting ageism, a pervasive phenomenon that significantly impacts both younger and older individuals. Young gay people often find themselves feeling marginalized and scrutinized, facing judgment for lacking sufficient experience or being labelled as "too naive" in their understanding of the community and its intricacies. On the other hand, older individuals frequently encounter dismissiveness, which can lead to profound feelings of invisibility and alienation within a culture that often prioritizes youth. This generational divide creates a complex layer of pressure, where individuals at both ends of the age spectrum are engaged in a struggle for recognition and validation. The expectations imposed upon them can significantly hinder the development of a cohesive sense of self, making it increasingly challenging for them to articulate their unique experiences and identities in a way that resonates with others. This ongoing tension complicates the quest for belonging and acceptance within a community that ideally should embrace diversity across all ages.

The tension between authenticity and expectation is particularly pronounced within the gay community. Many individuals find themselves battling against the pervasive notion that they must conform to a specific image in order to gain acceptance. For instance, those who are perceived as "too feminine" may feel immense pressure to adopt a more masculine persona to be considered valid or worthy, while those labelled as "too masculine" might face judgment for not aligning with what some people see as the typical characteristics of a bottom. This ongoing struggle can create a significant disconnect between one's true identity and the facades they feel compelled to maintain in social settings. The impact of this disconnect can be profoundly detrimental, fostering an environment where individuals may experience chronic dissatisfaction and a range of mental health challenges, including anxiety and depression, as they grapple with the dissonance between their authentic selves and societal expectations.

Internalized homophobia significantly complicates the ongoing quest for genuine self-expression and authenticity. Many individuals grapple with the internalization of societal prejudices, which can lead to profound self-doubt and persistent feelings of inadequacy. This internal conflict often manifests in personal relationships, where individuals may find themselves struggling to fully embrace their desires or to communicate openly and honestly with their partners. The pervasive fear of judgment from both the broader society and the gay community itself can severely stifle meaningful conversations about personal needs and preferences, ultimately hindering the development of deep emotional connections. It is crucial for friends and family members to grasp the significance of these complex struggles, as supportive and understanding relationships can play an essential role in helping individuals overcome internalized biases and foster a healthier sense of self.

Creating inclusive environments where all expressions of identity are celebrated is essential for fostering a sense of belonging. Friends and family of gay individuals must take an active role in challenging harmful stereotypes and fostering open, honest dialogues about identity and the diverse experiences that come with it. By cultivating spaces that prioritize acceptance, empathy, and understanding, they can significantly help alleviate the burdens that often accompany community expectations and societal pressures. Encouraging authenticity—regardless of age, appearance, or the specific roles individuals play within their relationships—contributes to a healthier, more vibrant community dynamic. In doing so, they empower individuals to embrace their true selves fully, which not only promotes personal well-being and self-acceptance but also fosters a more cohesive, supportive, and accepting gay community as a whole, enriching the lives of everyone involved.

Community Norms and Individual Identity

Community norms within the gay space often create a complex paradox for individuals who are trying to navigate their identities in a meaningful way. While the community actively promotes a powerful message of authenticity and self-acceptance, it simultaneously imposes a set of expectations and stereotypes that can be quite restrictive and limiting. For many gay individuals, these social norms dictate not only how they should present themselves to the world but also whom they should date, how they should behave in relationships, and even the specific sexual roles they are expected to fulfil. This pressure to conform can lead to significant feelings of inadequacy, self-doubt, or disconnection when one does not align with these established standards. As a result, individuals often find themselves in a difficult struggle between their personal identity and the desire for communal acceptance and belonging within the larger gay community.

The perception of what it means to be a "valid" member of the gay community can vary significantly based on factors such as age, appearance, and behaviour. Younger individuals may feel immense pressure to embody a certain type of flamboyance or hyper-masculinity that they believe defines acceptability within the community. On the other hand, older gay individuals often face ageism, being deemed irrelevant or out of touch with contemporary culture and trends. This generational divide can alienate members of the community, as younger individuals frequently look up to stereotypes and ideals that may not resonate with their true selves or personal experiences. Meanwhile, older members may feel dismissed, invisible, or marginalized, struggling to find their place in a community that often prioritizes youth and vibrancy. The complex dynamics surrounding age and behaviour significantly complicate the quest for authenticity, leaving many to question where they truly fit within the broader spectrum of the community, and making it increasingly difficult to forge genuine connections across generational lines.

Stereotypes surrounding sexual roles, such as the "top" and "bottom" dichotomy, significantly complicate individual identities, and experiences. These labels can create a rigid hierarchy that profoundly influences personal relationships and impacts self-esteem. Many individuals may feel intense pressure to conform to these predefined roles, regardless of their true preferences, desires, or individual identities. This pressure can often manifest in internalized homophobia, where individuals grapple with self-acceptance due to the heavy burden of community expectations and societal norms. The very labels that are meant to provide clarity and understanding can, paradoxically, become sources of considerable distress, leading to deep internal conflicts that hinder personal development, emotional growth, and the establishment of meaningful relationships. The struggle to navigate these imposed identities can ultimately stifle genuine self-expression and connection with others.

The impact of appearance in the gay community cannot be overstated. Judgments based on looks often significantly shape interactions and determine opportunities for social connection. Individuals who do not fit the conventional standards of attractiveness may find themselves marginalized, facing exclusion and isolation, regardless of their personality or character. This troubling phenomenon not only affects self-image but can also lead to various mental health challenges as individuals grapple with deep-seated feelings of rejection, inadequacy, and low self-worth. The overwhelming emphasis on physical appearance can create a superficial environment, where genuine connections and meaningful relationships are overshadowed by the pervasive need to conform to narrow aesthetic ideals that dominate social settings. This dynamic can foster a culture of comparison and competition, further complicating the quest for authentic acceptance and belonging within the community.

To foster a more inclusive and supportive community, it is essential to actively challenge these restrictive norms and wholeheartedly embrace diversity in all its forms. Creating welcoming spaces that celebrate individual uniqueness, regardless of age, appearance, sexual role, or any other characteristic, can significantly help alleviate the pressure many individuals face in their daily lives. Encouraging open and honest dialogues about identity, personal experiences, and the challenges faced can lead to greater understanding, empathy, and acceptance among community members. By advocating for authenticity over societal expectations, the gay community has the opportunity to evolve into a more supportive and nurturing environment that uplifts all individuals. This transformation would allow everyone to thrive without the burden of societal stereotypes, ultimately fostering a richer, more vibrant community where every person feels valued and empowered to be their true self.

Finding Balance in Personal Authenticity

Finding balance in personal authenticity within the gay community is a complex and multifaceted challenge that individuals often face throughout their journeys. As members navigate their diverse identities, they must contend with both external expectations imposed by society and internal pressures stemming from their own feelings and beliefs. The common mantra of "be yourself" can sometimes feel like a double-edged sword. While it encourages vital self-expression and individuality, it can also impose an unrealistic standard of authenticity that is frequently shaped by societal norms and community expectations. These pressures can create a significant rift between one's true self and the persona that is deemed acceptable or desirable within the community, leading to feelings of confusion and conflict. The struggle to reconcile these differing aspects of identity can be a profound and ongoing journey for many individuals.

In the quest for authenticity, many individuals find themselves grappling with limiting stereotypes that dictate not only how they should behave but also how they should look and identify. For instance, the labels of "top" and "bottom" come with their own set of rigid expectations that can easily pigeonhole individuals into narrow, often restrictive definitions of masculinity and femininity. This situation can be particularly damaging, as it may lead some to suppress their true desires and preferences, fearing potential rejection from their peers or the wider community. The pressure to conform to these societal norms can be overwhelming and stifling, especially for those who may not fit neatly into these predefined categories. This struggle often results in feelings of inadequacy, anxiety, and isolation, making it even more challenging for individuals to embrace and express their authentic selves.

Ageism also plays a significant and often overlooked role in shaping personal authenticity within gay spaces. Younger individuals may feel an intense pressure to adopt specific behaviours and attitudes to align with the expectations set by older generations, who have historically paved the way in the community. Conversely, older individuals may struggle significantly to find acceptance and validation In a culture that often prioritizes youthfulness and physical appearance over the invaluable experience and wisdom that comes with age. This generational divide can foster deep feelings of alienation and frustration for both groups, as each individual grapples with the complex notion of who they should be according to societal standards versus who they genuinely are at their core. The intertwining of age and identity adds yet another layer of complexity to the already intricate dynamics of personal authenticity, highlighting the challenges that arise when different generations attempt to connect and understand one another within the community.

Internalized homophobia significantly complicates the journey toward authenticity for many individuals. Numerous people bear the heavy burden of societal stigma, which can manifest not only in pervasive self-doubt but also in profound self-rejection. This internal conflict has the potential to impact personal relationships deeply and can also take a toll on one's mental health, leading to further challenges. The fear of being judged or misunderstood by others within the community can create a reluctance to fully embrace and celebrate one's true identity. This reluctance often results in a painful cycle of shame and isolation that can be difficult to break free from. It is essential for both individuals and their support systems to recognize and validate these struggles while actively working towards fostering a more accepting and inclusive environment where authenticity can genuinely thrive and flourish.

Creating supportive and nurturing spaces that fully embrace the rich diversity within the gay community is absolutely crucial for promoting personal authenticity and genuine self-expression. This process involves actively acknowledging and celebrating the myriad and unique ways in which individuals express their identities, ensuring that they do so free from the confines of harmful stereotypes, societal pressures, or unrealistic expectations. Family, friends, and allies play an instrumental and vital role in this important process by providing unwavering, unconditional support, encouragement, and validation. By courageously challenging societal norms and actively encouraging open and honest dialogue about identity, expression, and individuality, the community can cultivate an environment where all individuals feel truly empowered to embrace their true selves. This ultimately leads to a more inclusive, welcoming, and affirming space for everyone, where diversity is not only accepted but celebrated as a strength.

Chapter 6: Internalized Homophobia

Understanding Internalized Homophobia

Understanding internalized homophobia is crucial for anyone who wishes to provide meaningful support to a loved one who identifies as gay. This internal struggle often manifests as a profound conflict between personal identity and societal expectations, creating a complex emotional landscape. Many individuals within the gay community grapple with deep-seated feelings of shame or inadequacy, which can stem from pervasive stereotypes and cultural narratives that dictate how one ought to express their sexuality. These pressures can lead to a cycle of self-doubt and internal conflict. For family members and friends, recognizing and acknowledging these feelings is essential in fostering a more supportive environment. Such understanding allows open conversations about identity to flourish, ultimately strengthening relationships and promoting acceptance. By creating a safe space for dialogue, loved ones can help alleviate the burdens of internalized homophobia, encouraging individuals to embrace their true selves without fear of judgment.

The gay community, while often a vital source of support and camaraderie, can also inadvertently perpetuate damaging stereotypes that affect its members. Many individuals within this community feel significant pressure to conform to specific roles that are often defined by labels, such as being a "top" or "bottom." These labels carry heavy implications, leading some individuals to believe that they must act, behave, or even look a certain way to gain acceptance from their peers. This pressure can create a toxic dynamic, where members feel compelled to criticize one another based on their perceived adherence to these narrowly defined roles. Such judgments can exacerbate feelings of internalized homophobia, particularly for those who do not fit neatly into these categories or who wish to express their identities in more fluid or diverse ways. The result can be a community that, while striving for inclusivity, can sometimes become exclusionary, further complicating the journey toward self-acceptance for many.

Ageism represents a significant and multifaceted layer of complexity within the gay community, affecting individuals across the spectrum of age, both younger and older. Younger gay individuals often find themselves feeling dismissed or invalidated by those who have been openly part of the community for a longer period of time, which can lead to feelings of inadequacy or self-doubt. On the other hand, older adults may grapple with the perception of being seen as irrelevant or out of touch with contemporary expressions of sexuality and identity, leading them to feel marginalized within their own community. This generational divide can create a profound sense of isolation, where individuals on either end of the age spectrum feel they must navigate their identities in solitude, which in turn can exacerbate feelings of internalized homophobia. A comprehensive understanding of these dynamics is essential for family members and friends who aim to foster meaningful intergenerational support and solidarity within the gay community, bridging the gap and creating a more inclusive environment for everyone involved.

The conflict between authenticity and societal expectation can create significant challenges for mental health. Many individuals, especially those in marginalized communities, often find themselves caught in a difficult struggle between being true to their authentic selves and meeting the expectations imposed by their peers and the larger society. This internal conflict can lead to heightened levels of anxiety, depression, and various other mental health issues, particularly among gay youth who are still navigating the complex process of forming their identities. Family members, friends, and supportive communities play a crucial role in alleviating this immense pressure by actively encouraging individuals to embrace their authenticity and providing unwavering, unconditional support. Such encouragement can significantly mitigate the harmful effects of internalized homophobia and promote healthier emotional well-being. By fostering an environment of acceptance and understanding, we can help individuals feel more secure in their identities and less burdened by societal expectations.

Building supportive spaces is absolutely essential for effectively combating internalized homophobia and fostering a deep sense of belonging among individuals. By creating inclusive environments where all expressions of queerness are actively celebrated and embraced, families and friends can play a crucial role in dismantling the stereotypes and harmful narratives that contribute to internalized shame. This vital process involves not only actively challenging societal norms but also advocating for genuine acceptance within both the gay community and the larger society as a whole. Empowering individuals to fully embrace their authentic selves not only significantly benefits their mental health and well-being but also strengthens the connections and bonds within families and communities. This, in turn, promotes a rich culture of acceptance, understanding, and love that can have a transformative impact on everyone involved.

Its Impact on Relationships

The dynamics of relationships within the gay community, particularly among gay individuals, are significantly influenced by a range of external and internal pressures that can be quite profound. Growing up, many gay individuals encounter a barrage of societal expectations, stereotypes, and cultural norms that shape their identities and deeply influence their interactions with others in various contexts. This can create a complex and often intricate web of relationships where acceptance, love, and understanding are frequently overshadowed by the persistent fear of judgment or rejection from peers and society at large. These pressures manifest in numerous ways, from navigating the intricacies of romantic relationships to managing friendships and family ties, each presenting its own unique challenges that can be particularly daunting. As individuals strive to forge meaningful connections, they often grapple with the dual desire for authenticity and the need for social acceptance within a sometimes unwelcoming environment.

Stereotypes within the gay community can profoundly impact how individuals perceive themselves and relate to one another. The prevailing notion of being "too masculine" or "too feminine" often results in rigid classifications that dictate who can occupy which role in a relationship. This binary way of thinking fosters an environment where individuals feel an intense pressure to conform to societal expectations rather than freely express their authentic selves. Consequently, many gay men find themselves grappling with internalized homophobia, which can lead to strained relationships—not only with potential partners but also with friends and family members who may inadvertently reinforce these harmful norms and stereotypes. This ongoing struggle can create a cycle of emotional distress, further complicating their ability to connect meaningfully with others.

Ageism significantly complicates the relationship dynamics within the gay community. Younger individuals frequently encounter immense pressure to prove their worth and desirability, often feeling the need to conform to certain standards to gain acceptance. Meanwhile, older individuals may grapple with deep-seated feelings of invisibility or irrelevance, as societal norms often favour youth. These age-based biases can create substantial barriers to genuine connection, making it challenging for both young and older gay men to relate to one another on a meaningful level. This generational divide not only exacerbates the sense of isolation that some individuals experience, but it also hinders the formation of lasting friendships or romantic relationships that could transcend age-related stereotypes. As a result, the community risks losing valuable intergenerational bonds that could enrich the experiences of all its members.

The tension between authenticity and expectation plays a significant and critical role in shaping interpersonal relationships. Many gay individuals grapple with the profound desire to be true to themselves while simultaneously navigating the often rigid expectations imposed by their peers and the broader community. This internal and external conflict can lead to a façade of conformity that ultimately hampers the development of genuine connections. When individuals prioritize fitting into prescribed roles and societal norms over embracing their authentic selves, it can result in superficial relationships that lack the depth, emotional resonance, and fulfilment that come from being truly open and honest with one another. This struggle not only affects personal connections but also influences their overall well-being and sense of self-acceptance.

Creating a truly supportive environment is not just important but essential for fostering healthy and thriving relationships within the diverse gay community. By actively challenging harmful stereotypes, promoting inclusivity, and encouraging open and honest dialogue about individual identities and personal experiences, friends, family, and allies can significantly help individuals navigate the often complex and multifaceted nature of their relationships. Building safe spaces where all expressions of identity are not only welcomed but celebrated can alleviate many of the pressures faced by gay individuals, enabling them to engage in deeper and more meaningful connections with others. Ultimately, by gaining a better understanding of the impact of these dynamics, we can collectively work towards a more inclusive and accepting community that empowers every individual to embrace their true selves fully and build fulfilling, authentic relationships that reflect their identities.

Strategies for Overcoming Internalized Bias

Internalized bias can manifest in various ways within the gay community, often leading individuals to struggle with their identities amidst the pressures and expectations imposed by society. To effectively combat these deeply rooted biases, it is essential to foster a strong sense of self-awareness. Encouraging individuals to engage in deep reflection on their personal experiences and recognize the origins of their biases can significantly help dismantle harmful beliefs that may have taken hold. This process can be accomplished through various methods, such as journaling, participating in therapy, or engaging in open, honest dialogues with trusted friends and family members. By thoroughly examining how societal norms, stereotypes, and cultural narratives have influenced their perceptions, individuals can begin to differentiate between external judgments and their authentic selves, thereby promoting a healthier relationship with their identities. This journey toward self-discovery and acceptance is crucial for personal growth within the community.

Education plays a critical and transformative role in overcoming internalized bias. Families and friends of gay individuals should actively seek to understand and appreciate the complexities of gay identities, including the various pressures that individuals often face when they feel pigeonholed into specific roles based on pervasive stereotypes, such as being labelled as too masculine or too feminine. Engaging in workshops, exploring literature, and participating in community discussions can provide valuable insights into the rich diversity of experiences that exist within the gay community. By committing to educate themselves, loved ones can significantly enhance their ability to support their family members compassionately and effectively, while also challenging and dismantling the biases that may arise from misinformation or misunderstanding. This journey towards understanding is essential for fostering empathy and acceptance in their relationships.

Creating supportive environments is an essential and vital strategy in nurturing healthy identities. Friends, family, and community members can play a significant role in fostering spaces where open and honest discussions about identity and personal experiences are not only encouraged but celebrated. This can encompass a variety of settings, including family gatherings, dedicated support groups, or informal meetups where everyone feels at ease sharing their thoughts, feelings, and stories without hesitation. By actively promoting an atmosphere of acceptance, love, and understanding, individuals can feel increasingly empowered to express their true selves and authentic identities, free from the fear of judgment or rejection. This expansive support network can also provide a crucial buffer against the pressures of societal expectations, stigmas, and internalized homophobia, allowing individuals to navigate their journeys with confidence and resilience.

Challenging stereotypes requires active and ongoing engagement from both individuals and their communities at large. Actively encouraging the celebration of diversity within the gay community can significantly help counteract the harmful effects of internalized bias that many individuals face. This can be effectively achieved by consistently highlighting the achievements, experiences, and stories of individuals from a wide array of backgrounds, ages, and presentations. By displaying a rich and varied tapestry of experiences, the community can assist individuals in understanding that there is no singular or definitive way to be gay, which can ultimately alleviate the pressure to conform to narrow and restrictive definitions of identity that often exist in society. Embracing this diversity not only empowers individuals but also strengthens the entire community as a whole.

Lastly, prioritizing mental health is absolutely crucial for those grappling with the complexities of internalized bias. Encouraging open and honest conversations about mental health, along with providing ample resources for professional help, can significantly empower individuals to confront and address the emotional toll that biases impose on their lives. Families and friends should actively advocate for mental health awareness and support, emphasizing that seeking help is a powerful sign of strength rather than a point of weakness. By prioritizing mental well-being, individuals can work towards not only overcoming internalized biases but also embracing their identities in a more authentic and fulfilling manner, fostering a deeper sense of self-acceptance and resilience in the process.

Chapter 7: The Role of Appearance

Judgments Based on Looks

Judgments based on looks within the gay community frequently mirror broader societal norms and expectations, creating added complexities in the journey of self-acceptance for countless individuals. These judgments can manifest in a variety of ways, ranging from subtle comments that may seem innocuous to overt discrimination that can be deeply hurtful. This dynamic leads to a culture where one's appearance significantly influences social standing and overall acceptance within the community. For many gay individuals, particularly those who are navigating their identities during their formative years, these perceptions can be especially damaging. This environment fosters a damaging belief that conformity to certain aesthetic ideals is not just preferred but equated with personal worthiness and a sense of belonging. As a result, the pressure to meet these often unrealistic standards can take a heavy toll on mental health and self-esteem, complicating the already challenging process of self-discovery and acceptance.

The pressures stemming from looks-based judgments can be significantly exacerbated by the expectations that are often set within the gay community itself. Individuals may find themselves categorized as either too masculine or too feminine, depending on various factors such as their physical appearance and mannerisms, leading to feelings of inadequacy, rejection, and even isolation. This internalized pressure creates a complex paradox where, on one hand, the community preaches the importance of authenticity and self-acceptance, while on the other, it frequently enforces rigid stereotypes that dictate how one should appear or behave based on their chosen identity. The result is a continuous and often painful cycle of validation and invalidation, in which individuals feel an overwhelming compulsion to fit into prescribed roles that may not truly resonate with their authentic selves, ultimately hindering their personal growth and self-expression.

Ageism also plays a critical and significant role in shaping judgments that are often based solely on physical appearance. Younger gay individuals frequently feel immense pressure to embody a particular youthful aesthetic that is celebrated within the community, while older members may experience marginalization and exclusion due to pervasive societal preferences that prioritize youthfulness. This dynamic not only creates noticeable divisions within the community but also perpetuates a destructive culture of exclusion that can severely hinder the development of meaningful connections among individuals across various age groups. The inability to fully embrace and appreciate diversity in both appearance and age can stifle the richness and complexity of the gay experience, ultimately making it increasingly difficult for individuals to find the acceptance, support, and understanding they seek within their community.

Furthermore, the impact of internalized homophobia cannot be overlooked in discussions about looks-based judgments and their broader implications. Many individuals, particularly those within the gay community, struggle with self-acceptance, heavily influenced by societal messages that equate attractiveness with personal worth and value. This internal conflict can lead to a range of damaging behaviours, such as excessive social comparison or relentless self-criticism, which ultimately undermine mental health and overall well-being. For those who are already grappling with their sexual orientation, navigating these complex external and internal pressures can create a significant and heavy burden, complicating the quest for genuine connections and meaningful relationships. The interplay of these factors can hinder one's ability to embrace their true self, making it even more challenging to foster authentic bonds with others.

Creating supportive spaces that fully embrace diversity in appearance, age, and expression is absolutely essential for fostering a healthier, more vibrant community. Encouraging open and honest dialogue about the often complex challenges posed by looks-based judgments can play a crucial role in dismantling harmful stereotypes and promoting a culture of true inclusivity. By actively challenging the prevailing norms and celebrating the unique beauty inherent in each individual, the gay community can cultivate an environment in which everyone feels genuinely valued and accepted. Building these supportive spaces is not merely beneficial for individuals; it enriches the entire community as a whole. This collective effort allows for a more authentic, connected, and harmonious existence among all members, fostering deeper relationships and mutual understanding.

The Influence of Social Media

The rise of social media has profoundly transformed the landscape of identity formation and community engagement within the gay community. For many gay individuals, platforms like Instagram, TikTok, and Twitter serve not only as vital outlets for self-expression but also as dynamic arenas where societal norms and expectations are continuously reinforced or actively challenged. These platforms have the power to amplify diverse voices and unique experiences, creating a robust sense of belonging for those who may otherwise feel marginalized or isolated. However, it is crucial to recognize that these same platforms can also perpetuate harmful stereotypes and societal pressures, particularly among younger members of the community who are navigating their identities in an increasingly digital age filled with both opportunities and challenges.

The expectations surrounding how individuals should present themselves can often feel overwhelming, particularly for gay individuals who bear the heavy burden of societal judgments and stereotypes. Social media frequently promotes an idealized and often unrealistic version of gay life, which can marginalize and exclude those who do not fit neatly into specific categories or roles. For instance, the pervasive notion that someone might be deemed too feminine to take on the role of a top, or conversely, too masculine to be a bottom, can lead to significant internal conflict, confusion, and self-doubt. These societal pressures can originate not only from a heteronormative society but also from within the gay community itself. This creates a complex paradox, where the very spaces that are meant to foster acceptance, understanding, and belonging can simultaneously breed exclusion and judgment, making it difficult for individuals to embrace their authentic selves without fear of rejection.

Ageism stands out as a significant issue that social media brings to the forefront within gay spaces. Younger individuals often feel immense pressure to conform to specific aesthetic standards or behavioural norms that dominate online platforms, leading them to prioritize their appearance and social acceptance. Meanwhile, older members of the community may struggle profoundly with issues of visibility and relevance in a culture that frequently celebrates and prioritizes youth over experience. This complex dynamic can create a notable generational divide, where younger gay individuals might unintentionally overlook the rich experiences and invaluable wisdom offered by older members of the community, and conversely, older members might feel alienated or dismissed by the younger crowd. The pervasive fear of not being accepted based on age can significantly hinder the formation of meaningful connections and relationships, ultimately reinforcing the damaging notion that an individual's worth is inextricably tied to their appearance or strict adherence to prevailing community standards. This cycle can stifle both personal growth and community bonding, perpetuating a culture that fails to appreciate the diversity of experiences across all ages.

The impact of internalized homophobia can be significantly exacerbated by the pervasive usage of social media platforms. Many gay individuals grapple with the deeply ingrained belief that they must conform to a specific mold or set of expectations in order to be deemed worthy of love, acceptance, and validation from both their peers and society at large. This struggle often manifests in their relationships, where the pressure to fulfil certain predetermined roles—such as the top or bottom dynamic—can overshadow the potential for authentic and meaningful connections with others. Additionally, the relentless comparison fuelled by carefully curated online personas can lead to heightened feelings of inadequacy, self-doubt, and isolation. This experience can be particularly detrimental to one's mental health, as it creates an environment where individuals may feel increasingly disconnected from their true selves and from genuine relationships.

Creating supportive and nurturing spaces within the gay community is absolutely essential in effectively countering the pervasive negative influences that social media can exert. Families, friends, and allies play a vital and indispensable role in fostering environments where all expressions of identity are not only acknowledged but also celebrated and embraced. By encouraging open and honest conversations about the various pressures that social media imposes, we can empower individuals to fully embrace their true selves, irrespective of the often overwhelming societal expectations they face. By building inclusive and welcoming communities that prioritize authenticity over conformity, we can significantly help mitigate the many challenges faced by gay individuals today and promote a healthier, more accepting discourse around identity, belonging, and self-acceptance.

Redefining Beauty Standards

Redefining beauty standards within the gay community is an essential and urgent conversation that challenges the deeply entrenched stereotypes and expectations often imposed by both mainstream society and the community itself. For many individuals growing up as gay, the journey can feel like navigating a complex minefield of societal perceptions, where the definitions of masculinity and femininity come with rigid and often unrealistic guidelines. These prevailing standards can dictate who is deemed attractive or acceptable within the community, frequently leading to feelings of inadequacy and isolation for those who do not conform to these narrow ideals. It is crucial for families, friends, and allies of gay individuals to fully understand that these societal pressures can weigh heavily on their loved ones. This burden can significantly affect their self-esteem, mental health, and overall well-being, making it imperative to foster an environment of acceptance and support. Recognizing and challenging these standards together can empower individuals to embrace their true selves, promoting a healthier and more inclusive community.

The expectations surrounding age and appearance significantly complicate the landscape of identity for many gay individuals. There exists a prevalent perception that one must fit neatly into specific categories, such as being "too young" or "too old" to engage in certain behaviours or pursue particular relationships. This form of ageism can lead to young individuals feeling dismissed or rendered invisible, while older members of the community often grapple with feelings of irrelevance and being overlooked. The internalization of these societal beliefs can create a detrimental cycle of self-doubt, where individuals may come to believe that they are not worthy of love, affection, or acceptance, simply because they do not conform to the conventional mold of what is deemed desirable or attractive at their particular age. This ongoing struggle can deeply affect their overall sense of self-worth and belonging within the community, ultimately impacting their mental health and interpersonal relationships.

Authenticity becomes an increasingly critical point of contention when navigating the complex landscape of societal pressures. The widely embraced mantra of "be yourself" is often overshadowed by the intense expectations surrounding how one should express their identity within the diverse gay community. The pervasive belief that individuals must embody specific traits—such as adopting a more masculine demeanour to be recognized as a top or presenting a more feminine side to be accepted as a bottom—can significantly stifle genuine self-expression and individuality. This internal conflict creates a dissonance where individuals feel an overwhelming compulsion to perform a version of themselves that aligns more closely with community norms, rather than fully embracing and celebrating their true identity. It is essential for families, friends, and allies to provide unwavering support to their loved ones in embracing authenticity without being constrained by the often rigid and demanding expectations of society.

The impact of internalized homophobia can significantly influence the dynamics of relationships among gay individuals. When members of the community internalize negative perceptions about their own identities, it can lead to a range of unhealthy interactions in both romantic and platonic relationships. This internal struggle often manifests as self-sabotage, where individuals may find themselves projecting their deep-seated insecurities onto others or dismissing potential partners based on superficial traits that ultimately do not reflect true compatibility. Furthermore, feelings of inadequacy may cause individuals to avoid meaningful connections altogether. A supportive environment, cultivated by families and friends, can play a crucial role in mitigating these harmful effects. By fostering open and honest dialogue about identity, self-acceptance, and self-worth, loved ones can help individuals navigate their internal conflicts and build healthier, more fulfilling relationships.

Addressing the complex dynamics of power, particularly the dichotomy between top and bottom roles, is absolutely essential for fostering a truly inclusive community. The social implications of these roles often lead to entrenched hierarchies that further marginalize individuals who do not fit neatly into these predefined categories. By actively redefining beauty standards to encompass a much broader spectrum of identities and expressions, the community can move towards creating a more supportive and inclusive space for everyone. Families and friends can play a pivotal role in this transformative shift by promoting acceptance and understanding. Their efforts can help to create nurturing environments where all gay individuals feel genuinely valued and empowered to express their true selves, irrespective of societal expectations or pressures. This collective endeavour can significantly contribute to a richer, more diverse community that embraces all forms of identity.

Chapter 8: The Dynamics of Power: Top vs. Bottom

Social Implications of Sexual Roles

Social roles within the gay community often reflect broader societal expectations and stereotypes, which can significantly shape individual experiences, identities, and perceptions. The dichotomy of "top" and "bottom" roles serves as a complex framework through which many gay individuals navigate their sexuality, relationships, and personal dynamics. This binary classification, while providing a sense of structure, can create substantial emotional distress for those who feel pressured to conform to these predefined roles, particularly as they embark on the journey of defining their own sexual identity. The implications of these roles extend far beyond personal relationships, influencing how individuals are perceived, treated, and valued within the community and society at large, ultimately impacting their mental health and sense of belonging.

Internalized homophobia continues to be a pressing and critical issue, as many individuals grapple with the often overwhelming expectations imposed by both the larger society and their peers within the gay community. This persistent tension can lead to a damaging cycle of self-doubt and self-stigmatization, where individuals internalize negative societal perceptions about their sexual orientation and identity. Consequently, some may overcompensate by adhering rigidly to traditional stereotypes of masculinity or femininity, which can further exacerbate feelings of inadequacy, loneliness, and isolation. This complex internal conflict frequently manifests in various mental health challenges, as the heavy burden of these expectations creates significant emotional distress and turmoil. As individuals navigate this difficult landscape, they often find themselves trapped between their authentic selves and the pressures to conform, leading to ongoing struggles with self-acceptance and mental wellbeing.

Ageism in gay spaces significantly complicates the intricate dynamics of sexual roles and interpersonal relationships. Younger individuals may often face intense scrutiny for being perceived as too inexperienced or naive in their interactions, while older individuals might find themselves marginalized and excluded for failing to fit into the youthful and vibrant image that is frequently celebrated in gay culture. This pervasive age-related bias can create a pronounced divide within the community, where individuals feel immense pressure to conform to a specific image that does not resonate with their authentic selves or personal identities. The ongoing struggle for acceptance within the community often leads to deep feelings of alienation and isolation, particularly for those who do not conform to the expected norms dictated by their age or appearance, leaving them to navigate a challenging landscape of acceptance and belonging.

The pressure to maintain a certain appearance can play a notably significant role in shaping the social dynamics within the gay community. Many individuals find themselves subjected to judgment not only based on their sexual roles but also by how closely they conform to societal standards of attractiveness and desirability. This intense focus on appearance can lead to superficial relationships, where an individual's worth is often evaluated primarily by their looks rather than their character, personality, or compatibility with others. Such an emphasis on physical attributes can create substantial barriers to forming deep, meaningful connections among individuals. This situation perpetuates a culture in which individuals feel compelled to constantly strive for an idealized version of themselves, often leading to feelings of inadequacy and disconnection from their true selves. Consequently, the interplay between societal expectations and personal identity can have profound implications for emotional well-being and interpersonal relationships within the community.

Creating supportive and inclusive environments is absolutely essential for fostering a genuine sense of belonging among all members of the gay community. By actively encouraging authenticity and vulnerability, families and friends can play a significant role in dismantling the societal pressures that often accompany rigid expectations. Emphasizing the vital importance of individual narratives and personal experiences can effectively combat the harmful stereotypes that frequently dominate discussions surrounding various sexual roles. The ultimate goal should be to cultivate vibrant spaces where diversity in expression and identity is not only acknowledged but celebrated, allowing each individual to navigate their unique journey without the overwhelming burden of conforming to restrictive societal norms. This approach not only enriches the community but also empowers individuals to embrace their true selves.

How Power Dynamics Affect Relationships

Power dynamics play an essential and complex role in shaping relationships within the gay community, significantly influencing not only interpersonal connections and interactions but also individual self-perception, mental well-being, and societal acceptance. These dynamics are often deeply rooted in stereotypes and societal norms that dictate how individuals express their identities and navigate their social environments. The pressure to conform to specific roles, such as being categorized as a "top" or "bottom," can create an environment where true authenticity is overshadowed by the expectations and judgments of others. This phenomenon can be particularly pronounced among gay men, who may feel compelled to fit into these rigid and often limiting categories. Such pressures can lead to feelings of inadequacy, self-doubt, or internal conflict when they find themselves unable to align with these archetypes, ultimately impacting their overall sense of belonging and acceptance within the community.

The impact of these intricate power dynamics is further complicated by the pervasive issue of ageism, which manifests in a variety of ways across different stages of life. Younger gay individuals often face significant challenges related to their perceived lack of experience, which can lead to feelings of inadequacy and exclusion within the community.

Conversely, older members of the gay community may contend with a sense of diminishing visibility and relevance, struggling to maintain their place in a society that often overlooks their contributions. This generational divide can create an environment that fosters tension and competition rather than the solidarity that is essential for a cohesive community. The complex intersection of age and identity can lead to a profound sense of alienation, as individuals grapple with their place in a community that seems to prioritize youthfulness or certain specific expressions of masculinity and femininity over the importance of genuine self-representation and authenticity.

Internalized homophobia plays a significant and complex role in shaping how power dynamics influence interpersonal relationships within the gay community. Many individuals who identify as gay face considerable challenges in fully accepting their identities due to pervasive societal stigma and discrimination. This ongoing internal conflict can lead to a deeply rooted negative self-perception, which in turn impacts how these individuals engage and interact with others in their lives. The pressure to project unwavering confidence and to fully embrace one's true identity is often severely undermined by an underlying fear of judgment from society. This creates a difficult cycle where individuals may, perhaps unintentionally, perpetuate harmful stereotypes or impose unrealistic expectations on others that reflect their own insecurities and struggles with self-acceptance. Ultimately, this internal struggle can significantly affect not only personal relationships but also the broader community dynamics.

Appearance is an undeniably critical factor influencing the dynamics of power within the gay community. Judgments made based on looks can create intricate hierarchies that significantly dictate social interactions and the formation of relationships. Individuals who conform to conventional standards of attractiveness may find themselves enjoying more social capital and favourable treatment, while those who do not fit these narrow definitions may face exclusion, marginalization, or even discrimination. Such superficial assessments can foster a culture that emphasizes aesthetic appeal over individual qualities, talents, and unique traits, which further complicates the relationships that exist within the community and can lead to a sense of inadequacy or unworthiness among those who feel they do not measure up to these standards.

Building supportive spaces that actively embrace diversity and promote inclusivity is essential for effectively mitigating the negative effects of these pervasive power dynamics. Encouraging open and honest dialogue about harmful stereotypes, ageism, and internalized homophobia can significantly help foster a more accepting and welcoming environment where all individuals feel genuinely valued and understood. By recognizing and courageously challenging the rigid norms that dictate behaviour and identity, the gay community can work collaboratively towards creating a vibrant culture that honours authenticity over societal expectations. This approach not only allows for deeper, more meaningful connections among its members but also cultivates a sense of belonging that enriches the entire community, empowering individuals to express their true selves without fear of judgment.

Challenging Stereotypes

Challenging stereotypes within the gay community reveals a complex and intricate web of expectations that often contradict the very values of acceptance and authenticity that the community passionately promotes. Many individuals grow up internalizing deeply ingrained societal perceptions that dictate what it truly means to be gay. From an early age, they may encounter limiting ideas about masculinity and femininity that restrict their identities and their potential contributions to society. These pervasive stereotypes can create a narrow and often damaging definition of what it means to be "a certain type of gay," which can lead to overwhelming feelings of inadequacy, confusion, and isolation. In this challenging environment, the pressure to conform to specific roles and expectations becomes a significant obstacle, often making it exceedingly difficult for individuals to embrace and express their true selves fully and authentically.

The ageism present within gay spaces creates additional layers of challenge that can significantly impact the community. Younger individuals may frequently find themselves dismissed or underestimated solely because of their age, leading to feelings of exclusion. At the same time, older members of the community often experience marginalization or neglect, which contributes to a widening generational divide. This age disparity not only stifles meaningful connections but also undermines the development of robust support systems that are essential for all members. For young gay individuals, the societal expectation to embody a youthful and vibrant persona can be overwhelming and burdensome, while older members may feel an intense need to prove their relevance in a culture that frequently prioritizes youth over experience. Both groups navigate unique struggles related to their identities, often feeling alienated from a community that should ideally serve as a supportive refuge for everyone. This disconnect can hinder the growth of intergenerational relationships that are crucial for a more inclusive and cohesive community.

Authenticity versus expectation is a central theme that resonates deeply throughout the gay community. Many individuals grapple with the desire to be genuinely true to themselves while simultaneously trying to fit into predefined molds that society imposes on them. The pressure to conform to specific roles, such as being a top or a bottom, can overshadow personal preferences and desires, making it difficult for individuals to explore and express their true identities. This dynamic can lead to a sense of internalized homophobia, as individuals may judge themselves harshly for not living up to these rigid expectations set by others. The struggle for authenticity can become a battleground where the quest for self-acceptance is often sacrificed at the altar of community norms and pressures. This ongoing conflict can lead to significant mental health challenges that not only affect individual well-being but also ripple through relationships and the broader community, highlighting the urgent need for more inclusive and accepting spaces that celebrate diversity in identities and expressions.

Appearance plays a significant role in the judgments faced within the gay community, where looks often supersede personal attributes and character traits. The emphasis on physicality can create a toxic environment that categorizes individuals based primarily on their appearances, further entrenching harmful stereotypes that can lead to exclusion. This superficial approach can alienate those who do not fit the conventional standards of attractiveness or who choose to express their identity in unconventional and diverse ways. The resulting judgments can cause lasting emotional harm, reinforcing feelings of inferiority and inadequacy among those affected. This cycle of exclusion not only affects individuals but also perpetuates a broader culture of judgment within the community, undermining its foundational values of support, acceptance, and understanding. By prioritizing looks over substance, the community risks losing its essence and the very principles that should unite its members.

Building supportive spaces that celebrate diversity and challenge stereotypes is absolutely vital for fostering an inclusive environment for all members of the gay community. This not only includes promoting dialogues around the complex dynamics of power, such as the top versus bottom narrative, but also emphasizes how these roles significantly impact social relationships and individual experiences. It is essential for families, friends, and allies to actively engage in meaningful conversations that dismantle harmful stereotypes and encourage authenticity in every individual's expression. By creating and nurturing supportive environments, the community can empower individuals to navigate their identities confidently, without the burden of external expectations or societal pressures. This ultimately fosters a healthier, more inclusive atmosphere that genuinely values and respects every person's unique journey, allowing everyone to thrive and contribute to the richness of the community as a whole.

Chapter 9: Mental Health Challenges

The Weight of Community Expectations

The expectations within the gay community can often feel like a double-edged sword, providing a profound sense of belonging while simultaneously imposing rigid and sometimes overwhelming standards that can be incredibly difficult to navigate. For many individuals, growing up gay person involves grappling with not only societal norms but also the intense pressure to conform to specific identities or roles that may not align with their true selves. This pressure can manifest in various ways, such as the stereotype of being "too old" or "too young" to fit into certain molds, or the assumptions made based on one's perceived masculinity or femininity. The very community that passionately advocates for authenticity and self-expression can paradoxically enforce a narrow and restrictive definition of what it truly means to be a valid member of that community, leading to feelings of exclusion and confusion for those who do not fit neatly within these prescribed boundaries.

Stereotypes about age and appearance create a complex landscape where judgment often overshadows genuine support and understanding.

Younger individuals frequently feel the sting of ageism, as they are often dismissed as inexperienced or immature, leading to frustration and resentment. Conversely, older members of society may grapple with feelings of invisibility or being deemed irrelevant, causing them to feel marginalized and undervalued. This dynamic not only negatively affects self-esteem but also significantly contributes to feelings of isolation and loneliness. The relentless pressure to fit into a specific age bracket or conform to societal standards of appearance can lead to intense internal conflict. Individuals often struggle to reconcile their true selves with the personas they feel compelled to project in order to gain acceptance from their peers, resulting in an ongoing battle between authenticity and the desire for belonging.

Navigating identity within the gay community requires a delicate and thoughtful balance between authenticity and conformity. The mantra of "being yourself" can sound empowering and liberating, but the reality is that many individuals face significant scrutiny based on preconceived notions of masculinity and femininity that are often deeply ingrained in societal norms. The expectation to embody certain traits—such as being labelled a "top" or "bottom" based on one's perceived masculinity— can lead to internalized homophobia. This occurs when individuals start to judge themselves or others through a narrow lens of stereotypes that dictate their self-worth and value within the community. This internal conflict, fuelled by societal pressures and rigid expectations, can severely hinder personal growth and development. It may also foster negative mental health outcomes, as the overwhelming pressure to conform weighs heavily on those who feel they cannot meet community standards or fit into predefined roles. Such struggles not only affect individual self-esteem but can also create barriers to forming authentic connections with others, ultimately impacting the overall sense of belonging within the community.

The dynamics of power within the gay community further complicate these issues in significant ways. The binary distinction of "top" versus "bottom" often reinforces existing hierarchies, creating societal implications that extend well beyond individual relationships and personal interactions. This ongoing power struggle can cultivate a toxic environment where individuals feel compelled to assert their identity in ways that align with community expectations, often at the expense of their own true desires and personal authenticity. The impact of these complex dynamics can be profoundly detrimental, leading to a cycle of judgment, exclusion, and internal conflict that ultimately undermines the very sense of community and support that many individuals seek and cherish within the gay community.

To effectively combat these challenges, it is absolutely crucial to build and maintain supportive spaces that prioritize inclusivity and acceptance for everyone. By fostering nurturing environments where individuals can freely express their identities without fear of judgment or reprisal, the community can begin to dismantle deeply rooted harmful stereotypes and societal expectations. Encouraging open and honest dialogue about the complexities of identity, ageism, and the diverse expressions of being gay can significantly empower individuals to fully embrace their authenticity and unique experiences. Ultimately, creating a more inclusive and understanding community not only enhances the mental health and overall well-being of its members but also strengthens the very fabric of the gay experience as a whole, enriching the lives of all individuals involved.

Coping with Anxiety and Depression

Coping with anxiety and depression within the context of being gay can be particularly challenging, especially given the unique pressures that arise from both societal expectations and the gay community itself. Many individuals face a profound internal struggle, grappling with their identity while simultaneously dealing with external perceptions that can often feel judgmental or unaccepting. For family members, understanding this complex dynamic is crucial for providing support. The pressure to conform to specific roles—such as the expectations of being a top or a bottom or fitting into age-related stereotypes—can significantly exacerbate feelings of inadequacy, loneliness, and isolation among gay individuals. This chapter aims to shed light on these complexities, exploring the intricate relationship between identity and mental health, while also offering practical strategies for effectively coping with anxiety and depression in a way that promotes resilience and well-being.

The journey of self-discovery within the gay community is often fraught with significant anxiety, particularly for those who feel they do not fit neatly into established categories or norms. Young individuals may feel the heavy weight of societal expectations to present themselves in a particular way, conforming to the ideals of masculinity or femininity that are often perpetuated within the community. At the same time, older members might grapple with feelings of being out of touch, marginalized, or even irrelevant as the cultural landscape shifts around them. The perception that one must embody a specific type of masculinity or femininity can create an incredibly pressurized environment where mental health issues, including anxiety and depression, can thrive and exacerbate feelings of isolation. Family and friends can play an instrumental and vital role in alleviating some of this pressure by fostering open and honest conversations about identity, encouraging individuals to embrace their true selves, and promoting authenticity without fear of judgment or rejection.

Internalized homophobia is another significant factor that can greatly contribute to anxiety and depression among gay individuals. Many individuals grapple with deeply ingrained negative feelings about themselves that are rooted in pervasive societal stigma and discrimination. This internal conflict can create a debilitating cycle of self-doubt and shame, which further complicates the already challenging navigation of relationships within the LGBTQ+ community. By recognizing the profound impact of these feelings, family members and loved ones can play a crucial role in helping to create a supportive atmosphere where open dialogue is not only encouraged but normalized. Acknowledging struggles and actively affirming one's inherent worth can be incredibly powerful tools in combating the harmful effects of internalized homophobia, fostering resilience, and promoting mental well-being.

The role of appearance and social dynamics within the gay community is a crucial aspect that cannot be overlooked or dismissed. Judgment based on physical looks can lead to significant and often overwhelming mental health challenges, as individuals may feel they are being unfairly evaluated on superficial criteria rather than being appreciated for their true character or meaningful contributions. This pressure can create a pervasive sense of unworthiness, self-doubt, and anxiety that infiltrates personal relationships, making it essential for loved ones to actively emphasize the importance of inner qualities, personal integrity, and emotional depth. Offering consistent reassurance and heartfelt support can play a transformative role in helping those who are struggling with their self-image to find genuine comfort, acceptance, and ultimately, a sense of belonging within themselves and their community. It is vital to foster an environment where individuals feel valued for who they are on the inside rather than how they appear outwardly.

Building inclusive and supportive spaces is absolutely critical for effectively mitigating the mental health challenges faced by gay youth and adults alike. Creating environments where individuals can feel entirely safe to express themselves openly, without any fear of judgment or rejection, can significantly reduce feelings of anxiety and depression. Family, friends, and community members should actively strive to celebrate diversity in all its forms, reinforcing the important message that everyone has a rightful place and inherent value within the community. By fostering acceptance, understanding, and compassion, we can collectively work towards dismantling the numerous barriers that often contribute to mental health struggles. This will ensure that all individuals can navigate their identities with the confidence, resilience, and support they deserve, ultimately leading to healthier and more vibrant communities for everyone involved.

The Importance of Support Systems

Support systems play an undeniably crucial role in the lives of gay individuals, particularly as they navigate the often complex and multifaceted aspects of their identities within a community that frequently imposes its own standards and expectations. For many, growing up with a sexual orientation that diverges from societal norms can lead to profound feelings of isolation, confusion, and self-doubt, making the journey toward self-acceptance particularly challenging. Friends, family members, and supportive community allies become essential anchors in this process, providing emotional support, encouragement, and validation as individuals confront the various challenges associated with self-acceptance and societal perception. It is vital for those close to gay individuals to fully understand their unique struggles, especially the pressures that arise not only from external societal expectations but also from internal community dynamics that can sometimes be equally demanding and complex. Recognizing these challenges can foster deeper empathy and stronger connections, ultimately contributing to a more supportive environment for those discovering and embracing their true selves.

The gay community, while often celebrated for its inclusivity and vibrant diversity, can paradoxically contribute to the perpetuation of rigid stereotypes that add to the complex burdens faced by its members. The concept of being deemed "too fem" to take on a dominant role or "too masculine" to be perceived as a submissive partner can create a toxic environment in which individuals feel constrained and pigeonholed by their peers. This internal pressure can lead to a profound crisis of identity, where the deep-seated desire to be authentic clashes sharply with the overwhelming need to conform to community expectations. Support systems within the community can play a pivotal role in helping to mitigate these feelings by reinforcing the empowering notion that each person's unique experience is entirely valid. By promoting an environment where individuals are actively encouraged to embrace their distinctiveness rather than conforming to narrow, often limiting definitions of identity, the community can foster a more accepting and liberated atmosphere for all its members.

Ageism within the gay community significantly complicates the dynamics of support and understanding among its members. Younger individuals often find themselves feeling overshadowed by the rich and varied experiences of older generations, while older individuals may grapple with feelings of marginalization due to their age in a culture that frequently idolizes youth and prioritizes the perspectives of younger voices. This generational divide can lead to feelings of inadequacy, isolation, and fear of being judged or dismissed by others. Establishing robust support systems that effectively bridge these age gaps can foster meaningful intergenerational dialogues, encouraging individuals to appreciate and learn from diverse experiences and perspectives. Such connections not only enhance mutual understanding but also build resilience against the age-related biases and stereotypes that persist within the community, ultimately creating a more inclusive environment for all.

The impact of internalized homophobia can significantly affect relationships among gay individuals, often stemming from deep-rooted societal stigma and personal insecurities. When members of the gay community harbour negative feelings about themselves or their identities, these feelings can manifest in their interactions with others, leading to unhealthy dynamics and strained relationships. This internal conflict can create barriers to authentic connections and hinder emotional intimacy. Therefore, support systems must actively address these critical issues by encouraging open conversations about self-acceptance, mental health awareness, and the importance of collective healing within the community. By fostering a culture of understanding, compassion, and empathy, support networks can empower individuals to confront and overcome their internal struggles. This process not only aids in personal growth but also ultimately leads to the development of healthier, more fulfilling relationships, enhancing the overall well-being of the community.

Creating inclusive environments is absolutely essential for the well-being of all gay individuals, regardless of their perceived identity or appearance. Support systems should actively work to dismantle harmful stereotypes and promote authenticity over conformity in every possible way. This crucial process involves recognizing and celebrating the diverse expressions of identity within the community, encouraging individuals to embrace their true selves without fear of judgment or rejection. Furthermore, by advocating for comprehensive mental health resources and promoting awareness of the unique challenges faced by gay youth and adults alike, support systems can empower individuals to navigate their personal journeys with confidence and pride. Ultimately, fostering supportive spaces not only benefits individuals but also significantly strengthens the community as a whole, allowing for a richer, more accepting dialogue around the complexities and nuances of being gay. This collective effort is vital for creating a future where everyone feels valued and understood.

Chapter 10: Building Supportive Spaces

Creating Environments

Creating environments within the gay community is essential for fostering a genuine sense of belonging and acceptance among all individuals, particularly for those who may feel marginalized or pressured by societal expectations and norms. It is vital to understand that being gay encompasses a broad spectrum of identities and experiences, which is fundamental to dismantling the stereotypes that often prevail within the community. Many individuals confront various challenges based on factors such as age, appearance, and preconceived notions of masculinity and femininity. By acknowledging and embracing these complexities, we can work towards creating spaces that are genuinely inclusive, supportive, and welcoming for everyone, allowing each person to express their true self without fear of judgment or exclusion.

The pressure to conform to certain stereotypes can be particularly intense and pronounced within the gay community. Individuals may feel that they must fit into specific categories, such as being a "top" or "bottom," often based on their perceived masculinity or femininity. This binary view can alienate those who do not identify strictly within these limited roles, leading to feelings of inadequacy and internalized homophobia. By promoting an inclusive environment that values diversity and actively encourages individuals to fully embrace their unique identities, we can effectively challenge these limiting narratives and foster a broader culture of acceptance and understanding. This approach not only benefits individuals but also strengthens the community as a whole.

Ageism plays a significant and often underappreciated role in how individuals navigate their identities within gay spaces. Younger individuals, for instance, may frequently feel dismissed or overlooked, leading to feelings of isolation. Conversely, older individuals may grapple with feelings of irrelevance or invisibility, which can deeply impact their sense of belonging. Both of these groups face distinct challenges that can significantly affect their mental health, self-esteem, and overall sense of self-worth. Creating inclusive environments requires a committed effort to bridge the generational gap, ensuring that the voices and experiences of individuals across all ages are not only heard but also genuinely valued. This can be effectively achieved through the establishment of mentorship programs, fostering intergenerational dialogues, and organizing community events that celebrate and highlight the valuable contributions of individuals at every stage of life. By doing so, we can build a more cohesive and supportive community that honours the richness of diversity across age groups.

Appearance and societal judgment based on looks can further complicate the multifaceted experience of being gay. Many individuals face significant scrutiny regarding their body type, fashion choices, and overall presentation, which can lead to exclusion or discrimination not only from society at large but also within their own community. By fostering an atmosphere that prioritizes authenticity over mere appearance, we can encourage individuals to express themselves freely and openly without the persistent fear of judgment or rejection. This includes actively celebrating various body types, diverse styles, and a wide range of expressions of gender, ultimately promoting a more expansive and inclusive understanding of what it truly means to be part of the vibrant gay community. Emphasizing acceptance and diversity can help create a supportive environment where everyone feels valued and respected.

Ultimately, building supportive and inclusive environments requires a concerted collective effort to actively challenge existing power dynamics and foster a deeper understanding among individuals within the gay community. It is absolutely vital for friends, family, and allies to engage in meaningful

conversations about these critical issues, support
various initiatives that promote inclusivity, and stand
firmly against discrimination in all its many forms. By
doing so, we can create a nurturing and welcoming
space where all individuals, regardless of age,
appearance, sexual orientation, or identity, feel
empowered to embrace their authentic selves and
contribute to a rich, diverse, and vibrant community.
This commitment not only enhances individual well-
being but also strengthens the bonds of solidarity
that unite us all.

The Role of Allies

The role of allies in the gay community is absolutely crucial in fostering an inclusive environment that promotes acceptance, understanding, and empowerment for everyone involved. Allies can provide vital support to gay individuals who frequently face numerous challenges stemming from societal pressures and community expectations that can be quite overwhelming. The journey of self-acceptance is not only influenced by external perceptions but also significantly shaped by the internalized stereotypes and biases that many gay individuals endure throughout their lives. Allies play an essential role in helping to dismantle these harmful stereotypes, actively encouraging authenticity over conformity. This support allows individuals to express themselves freely and openly without fear of judgment or discrimination, ultimately contributing to a more accepting and diverse society.

Navigating identity within a community that frequently imposes its own set of expectations can indeed be a daunting challenge. Many gay individuals find themselves grappling with the immense pressures of trying to fit into predefined roles, whether it be as a top or a bottom, or conforming to specific age expectations that society often imposes. These roles can feel restrictive and may not reflect the true essence of who they are. Allies have an incredibly significant role to play in challenging these often rigid norms by actively advocating for a more inclusive understanding of identity that not only acknowledges but also embraces the rich diversity within the community. By providing unwavering support to individuals on their unique journeys of self-discovery and self-acceptance, allies contribute to the creation of a culture where being true to oneself is not only celebrated but also embraced, rather than subjected to scrutiny and judgment. This collective effort fosters an environment where everyone feels free to express their authentic selves.

Ageism is an increasingly critical issue within gay spaces, where individuals from both younger and older generations often experience feelings of marginalization. Younger gay individuals may grapple with the perception that their voices are not taken seriously or that they are dismissed entirely due to their age, leading to frustration and isolation. Conversely, older gay individuals may feel overlooked or judged for not conforming to the prevailing ideals that celebrate youth and vitality, which can result in a sense of disconnection from the community. Allies play a vital role in bridging this generational gap by actively promoting intergenerational dialogue and ensuring that the diverse experiences of people from all age groups are acknowledged, respected, and valued. This kind of support can foster a more inclusive and cohesive sense of community that uplifts and amplifies the voices and contributions of individuals across all age groups, creating a richer and more vibrant space for everyone involved.

The internal challenges of navigating relationships within the gay community are often further complicated by various external expectations and societal pressures. Internalized homophobia can lead to toxic dynamics that not only impact mental health but also significantly diminish relationship satisfaction. Allies play a crucial role and possess the power to challenge these harmful narratives by providing much-needed affirmation and encouraging open and honest conversations about feelings of inadequacy and self-doubt. By actively fostering a supportive atmosphere, allies can help alleviate the heavy burdens that accompany societal pressures, creating an environment where individuals feel safe and valued. This supportive approach allows individuals to form healthier and more meaningful connections based on mutual respect, understanding, and empathy, ultimately contributing to a more positive experience within the community.

Lastly, the appearance-based judgments that continue to persist within the gay community can lead to significant emotional distress for many individuals. The relentless fixation on looks can often overshadow the deeper essence of personal identity, making it increasingly difficult for individuals to fully embrace who they truly are at their core. Allies can play a crucial role in shifting this narrative by actively emphasizing the importance of inner qualities, character, and self-worth over superficial traits that are often highlighted in society. By cultivating inclusive environments that celebrate all forms of self-expression, allies contribute to fostering a more supportive and affirming community. This ensures that everyone, regardless of their appearance, identity, or any other distinguishing factor, feels genuinely valued and accepted for who they are.

Fostering Community Support and Understanding

Fostering community support and understanding within the gay realm is crucial for the well-being and acceptance of individuals exploring their identities. While the gay community is often seen as a space for self-expression and authenticity, it can sometimes also impose strict expectations and entrenched stereotypes that complicate the varied experiences of its members. Friends, family, and allies are vital in breaking down these barriers, creating an environment where individuals feel genuinely recognized and fully supported in their unique journeys. Acknowledging the complex nature of identity within the gay community can greatly aid in bridging divides and promoting a more inclusive atmosphere for everyone. By fostering open dialogue and empathy, we can work collectively to ensure that all individuals experience a sense of belonging and empowerment.

One major challenge that many gay individuals encounter is the significant pressure to conform to stereotypes imposed by society. Concepts of being "too old" or "too young," "too feminine" or "too masculine," can lead to intense internal conflicts regarding authenticity and self-acceptance. These pressures often stem from a strong desire for validation within a community that champions individuality and self-expression. As allies, it is crucial to understand that each person's experience is valid and distinct. Embracing a wide range of identity expressions can contribute to a more unified, inclusive, and supportive community for everyone. Promoting open and honest conversations about these pressures can be instrumental in dismantling harmful stereotypes and nurturing a culture of true acceptance and understanding among all participants.

Ageism represents a significant challenge within gay spaces, where individuals of all ages, both young and older, can often feel marginalized in different ways. Younger members may struggle with being taken seriously and finding their voices heard, while older members might experience feelings of being overlooked, dismissed, or even rendered irrelevant within the community. This generational divide can foster a sense of isolation and disconnection among members, which makes it all the more essential for family, friends, and allies to actively advocate for inclusivity and understanding across all age groups. By intentionally fostering intergenerational dialogue, community members can share their diverse experiences, knowledge, and wisdom, thereby enriching the community as a whole. This collaborative effort not only enhances mutual understanding but also creates a stronger sense of belonging for everyone involved, ensuring that all voices are valued and heard.

'Authenticity frequently finds itself at odds with societal expectations within the gay community, leading to a troubling phenomenon of internalized homophobia that can deeply affect both personal relationships and overall mental health. Many individuals wrestle with the notion that they must conform to a particular stereotype or mold to gain acceptance, which often results in heightened anxiety and pervasive self-doubt. Supportive allies play a crucial role in this dynamic, as they can significantly impact the well-being of individuals by affirming each person's inherent right to define their own identity on their own terms. By actively promoting the acceptance of diverse expressions of gender and sexuality, we can help alleviate some of the immense pressure that individuals face, empowering them to navigate their identities with a newfound sense of confidence and pride.'

Creating supportive spaces that prioritize inclusivity is absolutely vital for the overall health and well-being of the gay community. This process involves recognizing the diverse and varied experiences of individuals while actively working to dismantle the entrenched power dynamics that dictate social interactions, particularly the often problematic top versus bottom dichotomy. By encouraging a culture steeped in understanding, empathy, and compassion, family members and friends can play a crucial role in fostering environments where everyone feels safe and empowered to express their true selves. A community deeply rooted in support and acceptance will not only benefit individuals on a personal level but will also serve to strengthen the collective identity and bond of the gay community as a whole. This, in turn, paves the way for a future where authenticity and individuality are celebrated and embraced rather than scrutinized and judged.

More About the Author

Hannes van Zyl was born in Ermelo in the mid-sixties as the first of four siblings. He grew up on farms and enjoyed a healthy childhood. During his schooling years, he lived in a hostel, returning home on weekends and holidays. With his parents often away on business, he spent weekends with his grandparents and holidays with his parents.

After completing school, he joined the Prison Service, where he worked with death row inmates at Pretoria Maximum Prison, studied Psychology, and witnessed executions. After two years, he resigned and served in Panster, Bloemfontein, participating in final operations in Angola.

In the late eighties, he worked as a salesperson in Pretoria and, in the early nineties, started a business with a friend. He relocated to Rustenburg in the mid-nineties to launch a food industry business with his parents, later becoming an estate agent and furthering his studies in Project Management in the late nineties.

Hannes has built a solid professional background, leading high-performing teams with expertise in budgeting, timeline coordination, and risk management. His strengths include effective communication and the ability to collaborate with cross-functional teams while managing multiple projects on time and within budget. With extensive experience in construction management, he excels in project planning and innovative problem-solving, consistently meeting deadlines, staying within budget, and exceeding quality standards.

He is adept at stakeholder collaboration, defining objectives, and ensuring customer satisfaction, demonstrating a results-oriented approach in dynamic environments.

In his thirties, he took on the role of a father figure to two young men, ages 19 and 20, which transformed his life and provided him with renewed purpose. He is also a proud grandfather to three grandchildren. Tragically, his eldest son passed away in a motorcycle accident in late 2023.

As a Property Practitioner, he assists sellers and buyers in marketing and purchasing properties at fair prices, prepares essential paperwork such as contracts and leases, and collaborates with attorneys and lenders to estimate property values.

As a Life Coach and Public Speaker with 20 years of experience, he has helped over 300 clients set and achieve their goals, achieving positive outcomes in 139 out of 140 suicide cases, managing 126 child abuse cases, and realizing an 80% success rate in 189 drug abuse cases. He has authored seven self-help courses and delivered numerous seminars on transformative topics.

As a Project Manager and Director, he co-planned designs for various projects, successfully completing eight estates with 595 units, all on time and within budget. He also managed the construction of ten luxury homes, overseeing landscaping for these projects.

In his roles as a Business Administrator and Project Manager, he led teams in planning significant projects like a Retirement Village costing R 195 million and a 90-bed private hospital costing R 576 million. He redesigned a plot into a wedding venue in Pretoria for R 6,500,000.

His diplomas include Project Management, Business Administration, and Structural Engineering, alongside certificates in various fields such as Engineering Management and Public Speaking.

Throughout his life, he has maintained a passion for writing. In late 2024, he decided to pursue writing full-time, aiming to complete over 15 titles he has developed, with many more ideas and stories yet to come.

More Books by the Author

Heartfelt Obedience: Discovering the Blessings of Honouring Parents

The Bible places significant emphasis on the concept of honour, particularly in the context of familial relationships. One of the most well-known commandments regarding honour is found in Exodus 20:12, which states, "Honor your father and your mother, so that you may live long in the land the Lord your God is giving you." This commandment highlights the importance of respecting and valuing one's parents. It establishes a foundational principle that underscores the relationship between children and their parents, suggesting that honouring them is not just a moral obligation but also linked to the well-being and longevity of one's life.

In addition to the commandment in Exodus, the Bible offers various verses that further elaborate on the significance of honouring parents. Proverbs 1:8 encourages children to heed the instruction of their parents, emphasizing the wisdom that can be gained from listening to them. This highlights the idea that honour goes beyond mere obedience; it encompasses actively seeking to learn from parental guidance. By embracing this principle, children can cultivate a deeper appreciation for their parents'

Enduring The Silence: Stories of Hope by Scripture

As we embark on our own journeys of patience and trust, let us draw strength and encouragement from these timeless stories that continue to inspire countless individuals across generations. Each story serves as a reminder that even in our darkest moments, we are not alone; God walks alongside us, guiding us through life's valleys and difficulties. Even in those quiet moments when we might feel isolated and uncertain, God is working in surprising and profound ways, weaving together every experience, challenge, and triumph into a meaningful whole.

By choosing to move forward in faith, we align ourselves with His divine plan, transforming our waiting into a testament of hope and resilience that can uplift and encourage others on their own journeys.

Let us remember that our faith journey isn't solely for our own benefit; it serves as a beacon of hope for those who may be struggling to find their way in life. It illuminates the path through darkness and inspires others to seek truth and light in their own lives, fostering a deeper connection with the divine.

Beyond the Veil: Finding Hope after the Death of a Child

The death of a child is often regarded as the greatest tragedy one can ever experience. There is truly nothing more heartbreaking in life. In addition to the typical symptoms and stages of grief that many individuals face, various factors contribute to the unique and profound challenges of parental bereavement. The immense sorrow stemming from the loss of a child can be further complicated by a deep sense of injustice — the natural feeling that this devastating loss should never have occurred and that no parent should have to endure such pain.

Grief is an incredibly profound experience, one that touches the very core of our being in ways we often cannot articulate, especially when it involves the heartbreaking loss of a child. For many Christians, this journey through grief becomes deeply intertwined with their faith, offering a unique and transformative lens through which to understand the complexities of pain and loss. The nature of grief is multifaceted; it can elicit feelings of deep sorrow, confusion, frustration, and even anger. Yet, within these swirling emotions lies the potential for profound healing, personal growth, and a renewed sense of hope that can emerge over time. By acknowledging the intricate complexity of grief, we can begin to navigate our feelings with greater awareness while holding on to the promises and comfort found in scripture, which can guide us through even the darkest moments.

Behind Closed Doors: The Psychological Impact of Hidden Love

Understanding clandestine relationships requires delving deeply into the intricate and often tumultuous emotional landscape that accompanies loving someone who is already entangled with another person. For individuals who find themselves in such complicated situations, the initial thrill and excitement can rapidly be overshadowed by a multitude of challenges and emotional upheavals. The secrecy that is inherently woven into these relationships frequently fosters a profound sense of isolation, as lovers are compelled to navigate their intense feelings away from the prying eyes of public scrutiny. This hidden existence not only complicates the dynamics of the relationship but can also lead to a significant disconnect from one's true self, ultimately stunting personal growth and severely hindering the ability to form genuine connections with others outside the clandestine affair. The emotional toll can be substantial, leaving individuals grappling with feelings of guilt, longing, and uncertainty about their future.

Second Chances: A Journey Through Faith and Forgiveness

Understanding human fallibility is essential for everyone, regardless of age or background, as we handle the complexities of life and the myriad challenges that come with it. We are all inherently imperfect, prone to mistakes and missteps that shape our experiences. Children might stumble over their words while trying to express themselves, teenagers could make impulsive decisions that lead to valuable lessons, and adults may carry the weight of regrets from the past that inform their present choices. Yet, it is through these very imperfections that we come to appreciate the richness of our journey and the depth of our connections with one another. The Bible teaches us that all have sinned and fall short of the glory of God (Romans 3:23), highlighting our shared nature of fallibility and our collective need for understanding and forgiveness. Recognizing this profound truth allows us to embrace our human condition with grace, humility, and compassion for ourselves and others.

As we take the time to reflect on our shortcomings and the areas where we may have faltered, we also come to recognize the incredible and precious gift of grace that is bestowed upon us. God's grace is defined as unmerited favour, a divine love that forgives and restores us, even in the face of our many flaws and imperfections. In our daily lives, this grace manifests itself through the forgiveness we extend not only to ourselves but also to others around us. When we choose to truly embrace forgiveness, we create a vital space for healing and personal growth. Ephesians 4:32 serves as a powerful reminder for us to be kind and compassionate, urging us to forgive one another just as in Christ, God forgave us. This profound call to forgive empowers us to move forward in our lives, transforming our past failures and mistakes into valuable lessons that deepen our faith and enrich our relationships with others. By accepting grace and practicing forgiveness, we embark on a journey of renewal and connection.

The Silent Struggle: Understanding and Supporting Those Considering the End

Suicidal thoughts frequently arise from a complex interplay of emotional, psychological, and situational factors that can be difficult to untangle. For individuals grappling with these thoughts, it may feel as though they are engulfed in a deep, overwhelming darkness that obscures any sense of hope or joy from their lives. Many may become convinced that they are caught in an unending cycle of pain, with no possible escape, which can intensify feelings of hopelessness and despair. It is vital to understand that these thoughts often serve as a symptom of deeper underlying issues, such as depression, anxiety, or trauma. Recognizing this connection is crucial for seeking help. Moreover, it is essential to acknowledge that these feelings can severely distort one's perception of reality, making it incredibly challenging to see any viable alternatives to the pain they are enduring, leading to a sense of isolation and helplessness that can be overwhelming.

For friends and family members of those who are grappling with suicidal thoughts, it is absolutely vital to approach the situation with deep empathy and compassion. Many individuals may not openly share their feelings, which can lead loved ones to feel helpless and uncertain in how to provide the necessary support. It is essential to cultivate an environment where open and honest conversations about mental health can take place without fear of judgment or stigma. By encouraging individuals to freely express their thoughts and feelings, we can help demystify their experiences and create a safe space for vulnerability that may provide an invaluable opportunity for genuine connection. This connection can serve as a lifeline, reminding those who are in distress that they are not alone in their struggles and that there are people who care deeply about them.

In His Image: Discovering Personal Worth through Faith

Identity is an intricate and multi-faceted concept, shaped by a wide array of elements including personal experiences, core beliefs, and evolving perspectives over time. When considering the aspect of faith, identity transcends the mere social labels we might adopt; it is profoundly influenced by our intimate connection with God. For those of us grappling with profound questions surrounding our worth and purpose in life, recognizing ourselves as being made in God's image provides a foundational and transformative perspective. This divine image not only bestows upon us a sense of intrinsic value and dignity but also inspires us to embrace our unique identities in a manner that is both deeper and more meaningful. It encourages each of us to embark on a fulfilling journey of self-discovery and personal exploration through the enriching lens of spirituality, which, in turn, deepens our connections with God and with one another in a significant way. This journey invites us to reflect on our beliefs and experiences, fostering a richer understanding of ourselves and our place in the world.

Understanding spiritual identity requires a profound and nuanced exploration of the intricate relationship between personal beliefs and the teachings of various faiths. When individuals pose the question, "Who am I in the eyes of God?" they embark on a transformative journey of self-discovery that transcends societal measures of success, achievement, and value. This significant exploration is often profoundly informed by scriptural teachings, which emphasize the vital importance of recognizing oneself as a cherished creation of God. Embracing this perspective nurtures a stronger connection to one's spiritual identity and enables us to fully embrace our authentic selves. As we navigate the complexities of life, this understanding empowers us to live with greater clarity, purpose, and fulfilment, leading to a richer engagement with both our inner selves and the broader world around us. Through this journey, individuals can cultivate a deeper appreciation for their unique spiritual paths and foster meaningful connections with others, enhancing their overall sense of belonging and purpose in the divine tapestry of existence.

Surrendering to God: Embracing Peace Through Serious Health Challenges

The moment a life-threatening diagnosis is delivered can feel like a rupture in reality, shattering the world as you know it into countless fragments. For parents, *friends, and loved ones, the initial shock can quickly spiral into a whirlwind of emotions—fear, disbelief, anger, and profound sorrow. It is entirely natural to feel overwhelmed, grappling with questions that seem utterly unanswerable. In this heart-wrenching moment of crisis, it is essential to remember that you are not alone in this journey. The Lord walks with you in your darkest hours, offering strength, guidance, and comfort through His word. Leaning into your faith during this tumultuous time can be a source of profound peace, reminding you that even amidst the chaos and uncertainty, God reigns supreme and is ever-present in your life. Trust that He is there to carry you through the storm.*

As you navigate the tumultuous waters of a serious illness, it may be immensely beneficial to turn to Scripture for both guidance and solace during this challenging time. Verses that speak to God's unwavering presence, such as Psalm 46:1—"God is our refuge and strength, an ever-present help in trouble"—can provide the profound reassurance needed to face the myriad challenges that lie ahead. Embracing these powerful words can truly transform your perspective, allowing you to see your circumstances not merely as a trial to endure, but as a unique opportunity for deeper reliance on God's promises and faithfulness. Engaging in Biblical meditation can further enhance this vital process, helping to quiet the storm within and anchor your spirit in His lasting peace, providing you with strength and comfort during difficult days.

The Dynamic Property Landscape: Strategies for Success in a Changing Market

The South African property market presents a complex landscape shaped by a myriad of factors that affect both residential and commercial real estate. This market is defined by its dynamic nature, with constant shifts in regulations, economic conditions, and property trends. Real estate agents, landlords, and buyers must remain acutely aware of these changes to navigate successfully. The evolving legal framework, often influenced by local government policies, plays a critical role in shaping market conditions, impacting everything from property valuations to investment strategies.

In recent years, fluctuations in the economy have contributed to a volatile property market. The repo rate, set by the South African Reserve Bank, serves as a crucial indicator of borrowing costs, directly influencing mortgage rates and, consequently, buyer affordability. As interest rates rise or fall, the demand for properties can shift dramatically. Buyers must stay informed about these changes, as understanding the implications of repo rate adjustments can significantly affect their purchasing decisions and overall market engagement.

Distance and Disconnection: The Hidden Struggles of Christian Men Away from Home

The modern work landscape has undergone significant changes, particularly with the rise of globalization and technological advancement. Many Christian men find themselves in roles that require them to travel extensively or relocate for work, often resulting in physical separation from their families. This shift has created a unique set of challenges, as these men grapple with the demands of their careers while attempting to maintain their roles as husbands and fathers. The distance can lead to emotional isolation, making it difficult for them to stay engaged with their families and uphold their spiritual commitments, which are central to their identities.

For families of Christian men working far from home, the impact of absentee fatherhood is profound. Children may struggle with feelings of abandonment, while wives often bear the burden of managing household responsibilities alone. This dynamic can hinder children's spiritual development, as they miss out on the guidance and presence of their fathers during formative years. The absence of a father figure can lead to confusion regarding faith and values, ultimately affecting the family's overall spiritual health. The challenge lies in maintaining a sense of unity and shared faith, even when physical presence is compromised

The Power Dynamics: Exploring the Top and Bottom Division

The concept of "top" and "bottom" within the gay community often extends far beyond the simplistic notion of mere sexual roles, encompassing a much broader spectrum of identity, power dynamics, and interpersonal relationships. For many individuals within the gay community, these labels can carry a significant amount of weight, profoundly influencing not only how they perceive themselves but also how they are perceived by others in social contexts. The binary classification of these roles can create an environment laden with expectations and pressures, where individuals may feel an obligation to conform to specific roles based on various factors, including their personality traits, physical appearance, or age. This societal perspective can lead to a limited and narrow understanding of identity, ultimately constraining personal expression and authenticity, thereby inhibiting individuals from fully exploring and embracing their true selves.

Growing up, many gay individuals face an overwhelming barrage of perceptions from both within and outside the gay community. Young gay individuals often feel intense pressure to conform to societal archetypes of being a "top" or a "bottom," which are frequently dictated by stereotypes that associate certain personality traits and behaviours with these roles. For instance, those who are perceived as more feminine may be pushed toward the bottom role, while those who exhibit more masculine traits are often expected to take on the top role. This societal pressure can create a profound sense of dissonance for those who do not naturally align with these stereotypes, leading to internalized homophobia, feelings of inadequacy, and a struggle with self-identity. The societal call to "be yourself" can feel profoundly contradictory when societal norms impose such rigid and limiting expectations. This dissonance can further complicate the journey of self-acceptance for many young gay individuals.

When Shadows Wisper: Embracing the Devil's Bargain

Understanding the Devil's Bargain often requires a deep dive into the motivations that drive individuals to make choices that seem counterintuitive. It's essential to recognize that this concept is not solely about succumbing to temptation but also about the complex interplay of circumstances, desires, and the human spirit's resilience. Each of us faces moments when the allure of an easier path beckons, especially when we feel abandoned or isolated. Acknowledging this temptation is the first step toward empowerment, allowing us to choose wisely rather than out of desperation.

In many narratives, the Devil's Bargain symbolizes a moment of weakness, a choice made in the heat of turmoil. However, it is crucial to reframe this understanding. Life can often feel like a series of trials, and in those moments, we may feel that all hope is lost. The devil, represent the struggles we face—fear, loneliness, and despair. Yet, it is within this darkness that we can find the strength to rise above the challenges. Embracing the struggle can lead to profound personal growth and a deeper understanding of our values and what we truly hold dear.